Managing Your Boss
In A Week

Sandi Mann

The Teach Yourself series has been trusted around the world for over 60 years. This new series of 'In A Week' business books is designed to help people at all levels and around the world to further their careers. Learn, in a week, what the experts learn in a lifetime.

Dr Sandi Mann is Senior Lecturer in Psychology at the University of Central Lancashire and Managing Director of Advantage Psychology consultancy. She works with a range of organizations delivering training and consultancy in diverse areas including employee relationships, communications, stress and emotional intelligence issues. She is also a regular contributor to various national and international media outlets including television, newspapers and academic journals.

Managing Your Boss

Sandi Mann

www.inaweek.co.uk

Teach Yourself®

Hodder Education

338 Euston Road, London NW1 3BH

Hodder Education is an Hachette UK company

First published in UK 2000 by Hodder Education

First published in US 2012 by the McGraw-Hill Companies, Inc.

This edition published 2012

Copyright © 2000, 2002, 2012 Sandi Mann

The moral rights of the author have been asserted

Database right Hodder Education (makers)

The Teach Yourself name is a registered trademark of Hachette UK.

British Library Cataloguing in Publication Data: a catalogue record for this title is available from the British Library.

Library of Congress Catalog Card Number: on file.

The publisher has used its best endeavours to ensure that any website addresses referred to in this book are correct and active at the time of going to press. However, the publisher and the author have no responsibility for the websites and can make no guarantee that a site will remain live or that the content will remain relevant, decent or appropriate.

The publisher has made every effort to mark as such all words which it believes to be trademarks. The publisher should also like to make it clear that the presence of a word in the book, whether marked or unmarked, in no way affects its legal status as a trademark.

Every reasonable effort has been made by the publisher to trace the copyright holders of material in this book. Any errors or omissions should be notified in writing to the publisher, who will endeavour to rectify the situation for any reprints and future editions.

Hachette UK's policy is to use papers that are natural, renewable and recyclable products and made from wood grown in sustainable forests. The logging and manufacturing processes are expected to conform to the environmental regulations of the country of origin.

www.hoddereducation.co.uk

Typeset by Cenveo Publisher Services

Printed in Great Britain by CPI Group (UK) Ltd, Croydon, CR0 4YY

Also available in ebook

Contents

Introduction

The most common problem that employees in every working environment have is with their boss. Having a good working relationship with the boss is crucial to enjoying a positive and fulfilling work life, and those people who have problems or difficulties getting on with their boss can suffer in a wide range of ways: they might be allocated the least popular tasks; might have their ideas ignored and their creativity squashed; be sidelined or be passed over for promotion. Psychologically, they can suffer acute or chronic stress, poor self-esteem and severe anxiety, as they struggle to cope with the day-to-day traumas that can arise from a poor relationship with their boss.

Yet all this can be avoided, in many cases, by simply learning the skills to successfully 'manage' your boss. Most of us think that it is the other way around – that the boss manages us – but the astute employee knows that it works both ways. The employee should not be the passive recipient of the managing process. Instead, they should work hard to establish common goals, mutually beneficial ways of working and a deep understanding of what makes their boss tick, so as to best meet their expectations. If you understand how your boss operates, the inner working of their brain and their personality, you are far better able to meet their needs as an employee. And an employee who meets the needs and expectations of their boss will be a popular employee indeed!

This book guides you through the process of managing your boss so as to ensure that you are ideally placed to become their favourite employee. We start on **Sunday** by looking at the psychological make-up of leaders – these are the qualities that your boss, by virtue of being in a leadership position, is likely to have. From this general starting point, on **Monday** we then look more specifically at analysing – using diagnostic quizzes – the make-up of your boss in terms of their leadership and thinking style.

On **Tuesday** we take a different approach by examining the psychological contract that you have with your boss; this is the unwritten set of expectations that you may not even realize that you have, but which is vital to the success of the partnership. Once that is established, we can then look at how best to impress your boss on **Wednesday,** using body language and emotion management.

Once these basics are established, we can then, on **Thursday**, look at specific ways in which you might want to manage your boss; such as asking for a rise, seeking promotion or complaining about workload. Of course, sometimes you need to manage your boss because, quite frankly, they are the boss from hell, and on **Friday** we start to look at various 'hell'-type scenarios, examining ways in which even these bosses can be managed.

Finally, on **Saturday**, any issues not yet covered are discussed in the form of the most common problems about bosses that employees have approached me about over the years.

Sandi Mann

What kind of animal is the 'boss'?

The first stage to managing your boss has to be understanding them and starting to figure out what sort of person they might be. If you can appreciate and understand your boss, you will be far better equipped to manage them – it takes the guesswork away! Before we start looking at specific ways of diagnosing your own boss on Monday, we look today at the general characteristics that managers tend to have.

Researchers have uncovered quite a lot about the qualities of leaders – from the skills that a leader is likely to have to examining the things that tend to motivate your typical boss. This chapter, then, starts by looking at how your boss is likely to spend their day in terms of, for example, planning or communication activities, and what skills they are likely to employ (such as time-management, motivational skills or people skills).

We then start to look at more psychological aspects of the make-up of a boss, in terms of their attitudes towards their employees ('carrot and stick' versus 'co-operate and trust') and their own motivations at work – such as their need for achievement or power or even just the need to be liked.

Issues covered today include:

- Discovering what your boss does all day
- What skills does your boss have?
- Your boss's attitude towards you
- What motivates your boss?

What does your boss do?

Most managers or leaders take on a huge variety of tasks, and supervising you might be just a small part of their wide-ranging remit. An average manager will spend about a third of their time and effort on traditional management activities such as planning or decision-making, a third on communication activities (including paperwork), and the rest on human resource management activities such as motivating or training staff and on networking activities.

Knowing how your boss is likely to spend their time allows you a valuable insight into their mind, since you will have a better idea of the sort of concerns that may preoccupy them. This is important, since many people seem unable to see much beyond their own view of their boss in which the boss only performs tasks that are relevant to them as individuals. Yet only a tiny percentage of the work your boss does is likely to directly impact on you, which means that any tasks you perform for them or any requests you make will need to slot somehow into the broader world of your boss's remit.

This is worth bearing in mind on Tuesday, Wednesday and Thursday in particular when we will look at ways to work more smartly with your boss.

Qualities of a boss

In order to perform effectively in each of the above areas, your boss will need to draw upon a wide range of skills, including:

- the ability to allocate tasks appropriately among staff members
- the ability to project authority and to take responsibility
- excellent time-management and organizational skills
- ability to act on own initiative and be self-motivated
- skill in fostering team spirit
- motivational skills
- 'people' skills such as empathy
- communication skills so that they can relate and talk to people at different levels both senior and subordinate to themselves
- the ability to delegate.

These skills are ones that a boss can learn throughout their career, but many depend on an underlying psychological make-up. Not everyone aspires to be a boss and nor is everyone capable of taking on the role. Psychologists have identified several personality traits or personal qualities that constitute the 'make-up' of a manager and your boss is likely to have some or all of them. Understanding the psychological make-up of your boss will allow you greater insight into what makes them tick. They *should* be:

- **sensitive** enough to 'read' people and situations: they should be able to notice when people are unhappy at work or ready for more challenges, or when events might mean changes are needed in the workplace
- **analytical** and good at problem solving: many people turn to the boss for solutions and, although some of this will depend on training and experience, much will depend on an inborn aptitude towards lateral thinking
- **decisive:** even in school some children are able to make quick decisions while others are unsure of themselves and their abilities to choose a path correctly. The boss should have the self-confidence to go with any decisions they make
- **socially competent:** they should be able to communicate at different levels, to listen appropriately, draw people out and behave with suitable social etiquette in a range of scenarios

- **emotionally resilient** so that they have what some people call 'bounce-ability' – they can bounce back when knocked down and do not let this affect their confidence or decision-making abilities
- **proactive:** such people do not wait for things to happen or come to them, but actively try to make things happen or initiate their own projects
- **creative:** bosses are often creative people who are able to view things from various angles and come up with creative solutions or plans that stretch or go beyond previously established limits.

These qualities, then, make up the personality profile of the ideal boss. However, if your boss has *all* these qualities, you probably don't need to read this book! Not all bosses will, of course, be the same, and will vary in the degree to which they possess these traits. It is likely that the 'missing' traits, or those that are weaker, are the reasons that problems occur between employees and the boss. In addition, a great deal of the boss's managerial style will depend not only on personal qualities and skills, but also on their inherent attitude towards human nature and behaviour.

Your boss's attitude towards you

In very general terms, the way bosses treat people depends on their attitude towards human nature and behaviour. There are two opposing attitudes that bosses may take:

1 'Carrot-and-stick' attitude

The assumptions that a manager will make if they hold this attitude are that:

- the average person is inherently lazy and dislikes work
- most people need to be coerced, controlled, directed or even threatened if the organization is to achieve its goals
- the average person avoids responsibility, lacks ambition and works only for the financial security.

Bosses who hold these attitudes thus believe that rewards and sanctions are the only way to achieve organizational aims – thus their job is to be authoritative and directive.

2 'Co-operate and trust' attitude

On the other hand, managers who hold this set of attitudes towards people make the assumption that:

- most people are self-motivated to work and want to enjoy it
- coercion is unnecessary if people are given tasks that meet their own objectives as well as the organization's
- most people can be trusted to complete tasks without continual supervision
- people work for reasons other than financial security.

The boss that holds these attitudes thus believes that the best way of managing is to elicit co-operation from their team and create conditions that will ensure people want to work hard and achieve organizational, as well as personal, goals.

What motivates the typical boss?

Psychologists have identified five different dimensions that motivate or drive people in their lives. These motivations or needs exist in different amounts in different people so that one person may have high needs in one dimension but not in another. These needs are:

1 **The need for achievement (n-Ach).** People who are highly motivated by a need for achievement are concerned with accomplishments and compete strongly against others.
2 **The need for affiliation (n-Aff).** People who are highly motivated by a need for affiliation are concerned about establishing, maintaining or restoring close, personal, emotional relationships with others.
3 **The need for power (n-Pow).** People with a high n-Pow are motivated by a need to win a debate or argument, and to control or dominate others.
4 **The need for autonomy (n-Aut).** Adults high on the n-Aut are motivated by completing tasks without assistance from others.
5 **The need for activity inhibition (n-Actl).** People motivated by n-Actl are driven to do things for the greater good of an organization or even society, even at the expense of their own personal desires or needs.

So, which of these needs is your boss most motivated by? Successful leaders in organizations have been found to be most likely to have:

High n-Pow
High n-Actl
Above average n-Ach
Low n-Aff
Low n-Aut

That is, your average boss is likely to be highly motivated by a need for power or control, by a desire to act for the greater good of the organization and by some need for personal achievement. They are less concerned with building strong relationships with subordinates (i.e. you) or working on their own. However, it is important to remember that this is the profile of the *average* boss and that your own boss may have a different pattern of motivations.

Once you have a good idea of what motivates your boss, you will then be able to act in ways that concur with these motivations. For instance, if your boss is high n-Actl, they may expect the same from you and will not appreciate you appearing to put your own needs or goals before those of the organization. A boss with a high n-Aut will not appreciate unrequested input from you. And a boss low on n-Aff will not be keen to socialize with you or spend time and energy cultivating a friendship with you – so don't make them feel uncomfortable by trying to 'affiliate' with them.

SUNDAY

MONDAY

TUESDAY

WEDNESDAY

THURSDAY

FRIDAY

SATURDAY

Summary

Today, then, we have started on our journey to achieve a deeper understanding of the sort of person that is likely to become a 'boss' – a manager or leader. By examining the various ways in which your boss is likely to divide their time and workload, we have begun to develop an important insight into their mind and the day-to-day concerns that are likely to occupy them. As we have seen, it is crucial to see the wider picture that your boss sees – this is a vital first step to knowing how to work in ways that meet your boss's expectations.

We have also looked at the qualities that a typical boss is likely to have and these include being sensitive, analytical, decisive, socially competent, emotionally resilient, proactive and creative. This is not an exhaustive list and weaker bosses may not exhibit all these qualities, but being aware of any such gaps can be a good place to start understanding any difficulties that can arise. Finally, we looked at what attitudes to managing your boss might have as well as the sorts of needs that might motivate them.

Tomorrow we will look at how to carry out a more specific and in-depth analysis of your boss.

SUNDAY

MONDAY

TUESDAY

WEDNESDAY

THURSDAY

FRIDAY

SATURDAY

Fact-check (answers at the back)

1. What does your boss spend most of their time on?
   a) Planning, decision-making and paperwork ❏
   b) Networking ❏
   c) Attending meetings ❏
   d) Writing reports and other documents ❏

2. Which of the following skills are important for a boss to have?
   a) The ability to do as much as they can themselves ❏
   b) The ability to keep a professional distance from employees ❏
   c) The ability to delegate ❏
   d) The ability to take a slow and considered approach to making decisions ❏

3. What does it mean to be 'socially competent'?
   a) To be able to make people Laugh ❏
   b) To tell stories that illustrate ideas ❏
   c) To be confident walking into a room of strangers ❏
   d) To be able to listen and communicate at all levels ❏

4. A boss with a 'carrot and stick' attitude assumes that...
   a) People can be trusted to do their job properly ❏
   b) Most people enjoy their work ❏
   c) Employees need to be closely managed ❏
   d) Sanctions at work are rarely useful ❏

5. A boss with a 'co-operate and trust' attitude assumes that...
   a) Employees can usually be trusted to work hard ❏
   b) Most employees need constant supervision ❏
   c) People work for money only ❏
   d) Co-operation with staff is hard to achieve ❏

6. Authoritative bosses believe that...
   a) Rewards and sanctions are needed to motivate staff ❏
   b) Employees can be self-motivated to succeed ❏
   c) Employees want to achieve organizational goals ❏
   d) Staff can set their own work schedules ❏

7. People high on n-Aut...
   a) Are highly reliant on other people ❏
   b) Are motivated by power ❏
   c) Like to complete tasks without input from other people ❏
   d) Like to work with other people ❏

8. People motivated by n-Actl...
   a) Are concerned only with their own success ❏
   b) Are motivated by a need to please other people ❏
   c) Are driven to do things for the greater good of the organization ❏
   d) Are very proud of their achievements ❏

9. Successful leaders have...

a) Low n-Pow ☐
b) High n-Actl ☐
c) High n-Aff ☐
d) High n-Aut ☐

10. If your boss is low on n-Aff, they...

a) Will want to socialize with their team ☐
b) Are likely to join you for coffee ☐
c) Are not keen to spend more time that necessary with you ☐
d) Are quite argumentative ☐

MONDAY

What type of boss do you have?

Having spent Sunday looking at the general make-up of your typical boss, it is now time to get down to detail and have a go at working out what makes your own boss tick. Today, then, we focus on a more individual diagnosis of your boss – which is the first step to really understanding them.

There are many ways to classify or 'diagnose' people or their personalities and this chapter will take you through two of these methods. The first one is **Leadership Style** and there are six typical leadership styles which refer to the preferred way of managing that your boss is likely to use. The technique they adopt is likely to be chosen by them as a result of life experiences, training and personality. Knowing which leadership style your boss tends to use is vital in ensuring that you can adapt your own working style to suit their leadership style.

The other diagnostic technique is to examine their **Thinking Style**, which refers to the way that people process information. Again, understanding their thinking style will enable you to adapt your work in a way that meets their needs – which in turn will help you build a positive relationship with your boss.

The main features today, then, are:

- diagnosing your boss in terms of their leadership style and thinking style
- quizzes to diagnose your own boss
- tips for managing each type of boss.

Leadership styles

Leadership styles refer to the way in which the functions of your boss or manager are carried out or the way in which your boss typically acts or behaves towards you. The following are some typical leadership styles:

- **Dictatorial:** This boss feels that that they are in charge for a reason, that reason being that they are the best person for the job, and therefore their job as leader is to tell others what do and how to do it. Such a boss is often motivated by n-Pow (see Sunday) and finds it difficult to see things from other people's points of view. They tend to rely on reward and punishment in order to get the best out of their workers.
- **Bureaucratic:** This boss got where they are today by following the rules, and sees no reason to have a different philosophy now. They tend to lack entrepreneurial risk-taking qualities, but they are likely to be a law-abiding and reliable citizen who takes their responsibilities very seriously. Any queries from subordinates, problems to be solved or decisions to be made are dealt with by referring to the rulebook. Such managers like to have everything written down, and use forms and paperwork excessively to keep track of what's happening.

- **Charismatic:** This boss motivates their followers by inspiring them to achieve the organization's goals rather than pursue their own interests. This boss leads by personal example and is likely to gain great loyalty and hard work from their team. Such a boss is often himself motivated by a high n-Actl (see Sunday).
- **Consultative:** The consultative boss may be high on n-Aff (see Sunday) and is likely to involve and consult their team at every and any opportunity. Decisions are made with input from staff and changes to the status quo discussed thoroughly. Such a boss may be afraid of alienating staff or even of taking the plunge and making solo decisions – they may lack the courage of their convictions and prefer to share the burden somewhat.
- **Laissez-faire:** The genuine laissez-faire boss is the manager who observes that members of the team are working well on their own and need little input. The boss makes a conscious decision to leave them to it without interfering and is happy and comfortable to do so. He or she is likely to have a 'co-operate and trust' attitude (see Sunday).

Quiz to diagnose your boss's leadership style

Do your colleagues seem to vie for your boss's attention? 3

Does your boss often tell you what to do, rather than ask you? 1

Does your boss seem unable to make innovative decisions? 2

Do you feel that you can approach your boss about any problems? 4

Do you feel that your boss does not involve you in decisions? 1

Do you feel that your boss lacks creativity? 2

Does your boss show little interest in your views? 1

Does your boss contribute only when asked? 5

Do you often find that changes are made or practices introduced without your consultation? 1

Does your boss stick rigidly to the rules? 2

Does your boss leave you to get on with minimal input? 5

Do you feel that you want to work hard to please your boss? 3

Does your boss seem uninvolved except when problems arise? 5

Does your boss discourage you from approaching them with problems? 7

Does your boss often talk about visions and dreams for the organization? 3

Is your boss well liked and well respected by most people? 3

Does your boss involve you in most decisions? 4

Is your boss often preoccupied with other things? 7

Are there regular team meetings to discuss new issues? 4

Does your boss often appear inflexible? 2

Does your boss rarely introduce anything new without consulting you? 4

Does your boss seem uninterested in what you are doing? 7

Is your boss happy to hand tasks over to others? 5

Do you sometimes feel that you have too much responsibility? 7

Mostly 1s = Dictatorial
Mostly 2s = Bureaucratic
Mostly 3s = Charismatic
Mostly 4s = Consultative
Mostly 5s = Laissez-faire

(NB: your boss may not score highly in any one style but may be a mix of two or three styles.)

Tips on managing the boss according to their leadership style

Manage the **dictatorial** boss by:

- building their trust in you
- asking 'permission' before doing anything
- keeping them well informed with progress reports
- demonstrating that you are carrying out 'orders' willingly and with enthusiasm.

Manage the **bureaucratic** boss by:

- submitting any requests in writing
- not expecting any diversion from the rules
- supplying them with the rules when necessary to help them make a decision
- keeping written records of everything.

Manage the **charismatic** boss by:

- being enthusiastic about their dreams and visions
- demonstrating that you put the company before your own concerns
- showing loyalty to your boss and company
- demonstrating a belief in their plans and ideas.

Manage the **consultative** boss by:

- being keen to share in decision-making processes
- not being afraid to give your opinion
- giving them encouragement and praise
- involving them in social activities such as trips to the cafeteria at lunch or after-work pub visits.

Manage the **laissez-faire** boss by:

- showing that you can be trusted to get on with tasks
- sending emails etc. to inform them of your progress
- seeking help only when problems arise
- not bothering them with trivial concerns or issues.

Thinking style

Have you ever wondered why there are some people you can talk to and understand easily but others who seem to rub you the wrong way or who always seem to misunderstand your best intentions? These differences may reflect the various thinking styles we each have. Thinking style is to do with the way we prefer to think or how we process information.

In a ground-breaking book on thinking styles, Beddoes-Jones (1999) identified several different ways of processing information, leading to a variety of thinking styles. Many of these can be used to differentiate and diagnose the type of boss that you have, and enable you to work in a way that helps rather than hinders their preferred way of working. The following list shows some of the thinking styles your boss might prefer:

- **The detail-conscious boss:** Detail-conscious bosses prefer to process information in small 'bite-size' chunks. They are able to pay a great deal of attention to detail and are very thorough and tenacious. As well as having a preference to receive information in these small chunks, they also like to disseminate it this way, too – which can be frustrating if your preference is for larger chunks. The detail-conscious boss may think of time in days, weeks and months rather than years.

- **The big chunk boss:** Big chunk bosses like to have an overview or general impression of a topic and are less interested in the minutiae. They can become quite impatient if anyone tries to give them too much detail. This boss is good at thinking in the long term or developing an overall strategy, and is usually a fast processor simply because they tend to gloss over the less important details.

- **The left-brain boss:** Bosses with a left-brain dominance have a preference for order and logic. They are very organized and focused and like to finish a task once they start it. They also prefer to work on one task at a time rather than 'multitask'. This type of boss probably writes things down a lot and has excellent time-management systems such as in-trays etc.

- **The right-brain boss:** These bosses are big on multiskilling and will often be found doing several tasks at once. Things seem much more chaotic around the right-brain boss who may have an untidy desk, papers everywhere and be forever panicking over deadlines. They are forever forgetting things since they are not big on lists and rely on carrying information in their head – which is a mistake since their brain is less able to distinguish between tasks that they have done and those they have only thought about doing.

- **The reactive boss:** These bosses are thoughtful and cautious and preoccupied with the consequences of any decisions they make. This is why they often prefer to stay with the status quo rather than rock the boat with an idea or plan that might go wrong. However, they are good at responding to problems, needs or requests from their team, although they might require so much information before deciding on a course of action that subordinates become frustrated with the slow response.

- **The proactive boss:** Proactive bosses are initiators who love to start new projects – although they don't always manage to finish them before getting excited about the next one. In their enthusiasm to get going with a new idea or project, they may fail to survey the alternatives carefully enough, or pay enough attention to detail.

- **The sameness boss:** Sameness bosses like familiarity and stability so do not respond well to change. They have a low tolerance for difference and are likely to notice and reject what is new. This boss is likely to be older and have been in this position for many years, neither seeking promotion nor a new direction. They tend to be quite stuck in their ways and resistant to innovation.
- **The differences boss:** These bosses, on the other hand, embrace change and new ideas. They encourage fresh approaches from their team and are always looking for new ways of working. They are likely to move around, job-wise, a lot and constantly seek promotion and new direction. The differences boss may often reorganize their team but show little interest in mundane or repetitive aspects of the team's tasks.

Quiz to diagnose your boss's thinking style

Does your boss take a long time to complete a task, paying attention to every detail? 1

Is your boss easily distracted? 4

Does your boss prefer to work on one task at a time? 3

Does your boss often seem impatient when you are explaining things? 2

Is your boss quite cautious? 5

Does your boss resist routine work? 8

Is your boss very organized? 3

Does your boss dislike being disturbed while working? 1

Does your boss have a tidy and neat office? 3

Is your boss uninterested in the details, preferring the whole picture? 2

Does your boss insist on knowing every little detail about projects you are involved in? 1

Does your boss often seem to be doing several things at once? 4

Does your boss worry a great deal about the consequences of any decisions? 5

Does your boss tend to leave things to the last minute? 4

Does your boss like information to be cut to the 'bottom line'? 4

Is your boss good at repetitive or perennial tasks? 7

Does your boss get excited by the latest fad or innovation? 8

Does your boss delegate routine or mundane work to others? 8

Does your boss seem, at times, over demanding? 1

Does your boss have a regular routine? 7

Does your boss seem forgetful and need reminding about details? 4

Is your boss full of ideas? 6

Does your boss prefer to have time to think things through before making a decision? 5

Is your boss rarely late for meetings – and dislikes people who are? 3

Does your boss resist change? 7

Does your boss love to start new projects? 6

Does your boss seem less interested in finishing a task than in starting the next one? 6

Does your boss often have a vision or long-term strategic plan? 2

Does your boss always seem to be changing things? 8

Does your boss sometimes seem unable to consider the consequences of their actions? 6

Does your boss prefer to work on existing projects rather than to start new ones? 7

Is your boss unlikely to make snap decisions? 5

Mostly 1s = detail-conscious boss
Mostly 2s = big chunk boss
Mostly 3s = left-brain boss
Mostly 4s = right-brain boss
Mostly 5s = reactive boss
Mostly 6s = proactive boss
Mostly 7s = sameness boss
Mostly 8s = differences boss

(NB: your boss may straddle two or more categories.)

Tips on managing your boss according to their thinking style

Manage the **detail-conscious boss** by:

● giving them lots of information regularly
● making everything as clear as possible
● giving them lots of written updates
● not disturbing them when working and pre-arranging meetings.

Manage the **big chunk boss** by:

● giving them a general overview of projects rather than all the details
● trying to take care of the small details
● using bullet points or key points in reports
● talking long-term instead of 'day-to-day'.

Manage the **left brain boss** by:

● presenting thoughts and ideas logically
● arriving on time to meetings
● meeting deadlines
● not approaching them with too many issues or concerns at once.

Manage the **right brain boss** by:

● helping them with time management
● offering help as deadlines approach

- writing important points down for them
- giving them lots of gentle reminders of things.

Manage the **reactive boss** by:

- making sure they are fully informed
- helping them think through any consequences of any decisions you want them to make
- giving them plenty of time and space to make decisions
- showing that you have considered every eventuality

Manage the **proactive boss** by:

- approaching them with exciting new ideas
- helping them to complete tasks they get 'bored' with
- getting excited by their ideas
- surveying all the alternatives – so they don't have to.

Manage the **sameness boss** by:

- pointing out how new tasks are similar to old ones
- helping with decision-making by reminding them of a previous precedent
- resisting the temptation to suggest a lot of new ideas
- helping them cope with change by suggesting a gradual change rather than a quantum leap.

Manage the **differences boss** by:

- pointing out how different new ideas are from old ones
- thinking laterally
- bringing new ideas to their attention
- reacting positively to change.

For more on thinking styles, including a full questionnaire on diagnosing your own thinking style, contact BJA Associates Ltd (website: www.thinkingstyles.co.uk). *Thinking Styles: Relationships That Work* is published by BJA Associates (1999).

Summary

Today we have used two techniques to diagnose your boss – Leadership Styles and Thinking Styles. Using the **Leadership Style** quiz, you have been able to work out whether your boss is a dictatorial, bureaucratic, charismatic, consultative, or laissez-faire boss – and, most importantly, you can use the tips given today to manage your boss according to their leadership styles. Leadership Style is, however, only one way of diagnosing your boss and we have also looked at **Thinking Style** in order to ascertain whether your boss is detail-conscious, big chunk, left brain, right brain, reactive, proactive, sameness or differences focused.

It is a good idea to keep a note of your boss's diagnostic type, using the quizzes in this chapter, together with the specific tips suggested to deal with that type. This way you will have this information to refer to and will be able to build on this throughout the rest of the book. You should bear in mind that sometimes an individual does not fit neatly into a category and may straddle two or three. Either way, you should now be equipped with the knowledge you need to really start managing your boss effectively by meeting their expectations and needs; this is a theme that is continued tomorrow when we look at the psychological contract.

SUNDAY
MONDAY
TUESDAY
WEDNESDAY
THURSDAY
FRIDAY
SATURDAY

Fact-check (answers at the back)

1. The dictatorial boss is motivated by...
   a) N-Pow ❏
   b) N-Aut ❏
   c) N-Aff ❏
   d) N-Actl ❏

2. The bureaucratic boss should *not* be managed by...
   a) Submitting material in writing ❏
   b) Sticking to the rules ❏
   c) Taking risks ❏
   d) Keeping records and notes ❏

3. The charismatic boss is *not* likely to...
   a) Inspire people ❏
   b) Lead by personal example, ❏
   c) Be motivated by high n-Pow ❏
   d) Inspire great loyalty ❏

4. The consultative boss can be managed by:
   a) Expecting them to make the decisions themselves ❏
   b) Keeping your opinions to yourself ❏
   c) Avoiding opportunities for social interaction ❏
   d) Giving them encouragement and praise ❏

5. The laissez-faire boss tends to...
   a) Be heavily involved in employee work ❏
   b) Want to know what you are doing at all times ❏
   c) Have a 'co-operate and trust' attitude ❏
   d) Not be available to deal with any problems ❏

6. You should *not* manage the laissez-faire boss by...

   a) Seeking reassurance over everything ❏
   b) Turning to others for input where possible ❏
   c) Putting problems in writing ❏
   d) Requesting formal meetings to discuss issues ❏

7. The detail-conscious boss differs from the big chunk boss in that they are more likely to...
   a) Prefer their reports with subheadings and sections ❏
   b) Be happy to be interrupted when working ❏
   c) Prefer an overview of projects rather than the minor details ❏
   d) Look at the longer-term picture ❏

8. The right-brain boss is more likely than the left brain boss to...
   a) Like order and logic ❏
   b) Be doing several tasks at once ❏
   c) Have a tidy desk ❏
   d) Be organized ❏

9. The reactive boss is more likely to than the proactive boss to...
   a) Start new projects ❏
   b) Fail to consider the alternatives ❏
   c) Make impulsive decisions ❏
   d) Take a long time making decisions ❏

10. Unlike the sameness boss, the differences boss...
    a) Likes things to stay the same ❏
    b) Is reluctant to adopt new ideas ❏
    c) Dislikes the mundane or repetitive parts of a job ❏
    d) Is likely to be resistant to new ways of working ❏

TUESDAY

Using the psychological contract to manage your boss

Having spent the last two days analysing your boss, you should now be well aware of what makes them tick. Today we build on this knowledge by examining the 'psychological' contract that you have with them. You may not even be aware that you have such a contract, but this informal contract forms the basis on which the working relationship with your boss stands.

The **psychological contract** is the unwritten and informal set of agreements about the expectations that you and your boss will have, consciously or not, about your job and roles. It is different from the more formal written contract in that it is not explicit and is not binding. However, it covers those important elements of work life that can make the difference between getting on with your boss or not. These include establishing optimal ways of communicating with your boss (including frequency, media, format, etc.); patterns of working (e.g. working from home, flexi-working, etc.), level of proactivity (does your boss expect you to be proactive or reactive with work projects?) and professional development (e.g. training opportunities that can give you key transferrable skills).

The day will end by looking at ways to best establish the psychological contract by covering the above areas, in order to meet mutual expectations between you and your boss

Topics today thus include:

● communications
● progress reports
● working patterns
● level of proactivity
● professional development
● how to establish the psychological contract.

Communications

The whole key to managing your boss is to meet their expectations – make *them* happy and they will be best inclined to keep *you* happy. Communication is a key area and managing this aspect can make or break your relationship with the boss. When you are establishing your psychological contract, you should aim to have the following questions answered:

- Which mode of communication does your boss prefer?
- How frequently does your boss want to hear from you?
- Does your boss want to hear about every issue or just major problems?
- How does your boss want to hear about your achievements?
- How can you expect to receive communications from your boss?
- Does your boss expect responses to every communication?

Mode of communication

The communication medium that your boss prefers may depend on what you wish to communicate. The choices are phone (including voicemail), face-to-face (which can be in an arranged meeting or on an ad hoc, by-the-coffee-machine basis), written memo or email. It is important to establish the preferred medium before you start bombarding your boss with daily emails, only to find they never log on or receive 120 emails a day. As a general rule, use the guide in Table 1.

Table 1   Modes of communication

Medium	Best for ...	Psychological contract: check that...
Phone	important issues requiring an immediate response.	...your boss doesn't mind being disturbed at such times.
Email	queries that don't need a quick response, issues you want your boss to be aware of (including your achievements) and of which you are happy for there to be a written record. (You should be aware that emails can end up printed off and put in your file.)	...your boss uses email but doesn't get so many that there is no time to read them all.
Memo	when you want to use a different medium from your usual one to emphasize a point (memos should not be used frequently). Also used to attach to another document or report you are submitting.	...your boss does not dislike bits of paper floating around and clogging their in-tray.
Formal meeting	complex issues that need face-to-face contact.	...your boss expects the occasional face-to-face meeting and will make time for you when you request one.
Ad hoc face-to-face	quick, on-the-spur issues that arise just as the boss appears.	...your boss doesn't mind being 'hassled' every time they wander down to the canteen.

Progress reports

For this section, it will help to refer back to Monday in order to understand what kind of boss you have. Your boss's attitude to progress reports and updates will probably depend largely on their leadership and thinking style.

However, the beauty of establishing a psychological contract is that this is one area where you do not need to use guesswork – you can simply ask your boss. And ask them you must, since this is an area that can lead many a boss to lose confidence in their workers since they may feel that they do not know what their staff are doing.

When it comes to information concerning the progress of projects, there are generally three types of boss:

1 the boss who wants to be kept informed at every stage
2 the boss who is happy just to receive the finished product
3 the boss who likes occasional updates.

Find out, during the psychological contract-setting stage, what kind of boss yours is – so that you can meet their expectations. Once you know about the expected frequency of communication, you will need to establish the preferred medium of communication – and this may be different for progress reports than for other types of communication. For instance, many a boss who prefers emails for general communication purposes expects formally typed reports when it comes to updates on progress.

Working patterns

Unless your official contract is very specific about your required working pattern (and many jobs now do not have strictly defined hours – the days of clocking on and off are gone for many skilled workers), your psychological contract should cover these aspects. Certainly, with new patterns of working becoming more and more popular, the chances are that you will need to suss out and agree some answers to the following questions:

- Am I expected to be in the office at a particular time in the morning?
- Am I expected to be at my desk by a particular time?
- Am I expected to work late and, if so, how often?
- Am I expected to work weekends?
- Are my hours flexible?
- Can I work from home (if so, how often)?
- If I am not at my desk (e.g. out with a client), am I expected to tell you where I am?
- Do you want to know my whereabouts at all times in advance?

It should be stressed here that most of these questions should not be asked explicitly since there may not be any easy answers your boss can give. Rather, they are questions that you should be attempting to find answers to during the process of establishing the psychological contract that will be discussed later. In addition, explicit answers may not tell the whole story. For instance, a boss may say that working late is not necessary, but may be secretly impressed by the late-worker. It is your task to find the real answers, not the given ones. In general, you should be aware of the issues outlined in Table 2 below regarding working patterns when establishing your psychological contract (see also tomorrow's material on impressing your boss).

Table 2　Working patterns

Arriving early	The boss is usually impressed by this since it demonstrates how hard-working you are. But be aware that a psychological contract is two-way and it might not suit you to be up at the crack of dawn every day. Come to some compromise with yourself. (NB: check that your boss is in to witness your early starts if this is the whole point of them!)
Working late	The boss is likely to be impressed again, but be careful. Working late too often can lead many bosses to think that you are a slow or inefficient worker. Find the right balance.
Working weekends	This a point that can be explicitly agreed between you and your boss. See Thursday's material on the rights you have regarding weekend work.
Flexi-hours	Many workers love the idea of flexi-hours; for instance, they can avoid the rush-hour or can do the school-run. But, be careful that your flexible hours do not compromise your visibility – make sure you do not miss meetings or key events that might happen before you arrive.
Working from home	The main thing to be aware of here is visibility – if you are home-based for some or all of the week, you are not around to be seen to be working or for informal but valuable networking opportunities. Your boss may say they are OK with your being home-based but may feel insecure about what you are doing when you are out of sight. Counter this by agreeing within the psychological contract to keep your boss more informed of progress than an office-based worker.
Diaries	Keeping these either in advance or retrospectively is a good idea. If your boss does not want them, agree within your psychological contract that you will keep hold of them yourself. They are a valuable record of what you have been doing and when, especially if yours is not the sort of job with easily measured work outputs.

Level of proactivity

How proactive does your boss expect you to be? And does this match the level of proactivity that you would like in your job? These are the sorts of questions you need to find answers to within your psychological contract. Some bosses expect their staff to sit in their cubicle and wait for the work to come to them. Such bosses do not encourage creativity and innovation and are probably found within the sort of industry where routine and mundane tasks make up the bulk of the work. On the other hand, more and more bosses expect staff to be proactive to some degree and go out and find work or look for ways of improving the status quo.

Similarly, some employees would rather just get on with tasks assigned without having to worry about being proactive while others feel that this would stifle their creativity. Establish the level of proactivity your boss desires according to the following hierarchy:

Level 1   **Total reactivity.** Here the boss expects you to complete assigned tasks only. No need for proactivity.

Level 2   **Reluctant proactivity.** Here the boss will allow you to be proactive only when your assigned tasks are completed.

Level 3   **Partial proactivity.** This boss encourages proactivity, although a reasonable portion of work will be assigned tasks that must be completed as well.

Level 4   **Majority proactivity.** Here, it is expected that most of your work will be self-generated with only the occasional task being assigned by the boss. Very often, the level of proactivity the boss expects will be implicit rather than explicitly stated; this is why the psychological contract is so important since it helps bring implicit expectations to the forefront of consciousness.

Professional development

It is in the area of personal professional development that the concept of a psychological contract is most widely known. Historically, the whole idea of a psychological contract was tied up with the expectations an employee had of the employer in terms of career development – i.e., I will work hard for you and in return you will give me reasonable job security, promotion prospects and the skills to make me marketable to other firms. This contract has changed dramatically over the years as the idea of jobs for life has disintegrated with the advent of downsizing, globalization and increased competition from new markets. Now, it is unreasonable to expect your employer either to offer you a job for life, or even to manage your career development. Instead, a new psychological contract should be drawn up in which the employee pledges to take responsibility for their own career development while the employer agrees to provide the employee with the training or experiences necessary to make them marketable.

It is thus important to get your boss to commit to helping you with your continuing professional development. For your part, you should identify gaps in your skill, knowledge or experience base and look for opportunities to fill those gaps. The aim with your psychological contract is to gain your boss's consent for you to take up these opportunities through attendance of training courses, contributing to or performing new tasks, or learning new skills.

Establishing the psychological contract

Now that we know what a psychological contract should consist of, we can turn our attention to devising or establishing such a contract. The important point to remember is that the psychological contract differs from the formal contract in that:

- it is not explicit
- it is rarely written
- it is very informal
- it may not be established prior to starting the job or even within the first few weeks
- it is not binding
- it has no legal element.

The process of establishing the psychological contract can begin when you start a new job but, equally, can be started at any point. Use the following guide to help:

How to develop your psychological contract

● **Step 1:** Begin by making a list of the areas to be agreed upon or questions you need answers to, using the material discussed earlier in this section. You might want to create a table or just itemize areas in a note-pad. You will need to write down areas such as 'communications' (see earlier section for a suggested list of questions), 'progress reports', 'working patterns' (again, some suggested questions are discussed earlier today) and 'level of proactivity'. Next to each item, you can make your own notes as and when you find the answers. Allow yourself a three-month period to get all the answers.

● **Step 2:** Start trying to fill in your table or finding answers to your questions by asking or observing. Some things will be appropriate to take up with your boss but for others you could try asking colleagues who have been there longer or know your boss better. Other issues will be resolved simply by seeing how your boss behaves and inferring what they expect from that.

● **Step 3:** Constantly review your psychological contract once you have completed it. Expectations change, especially in today's turbulent business climate. New staff, new technology and new patterns of working can all mean your psychological contract will need reviewing.

SUNDAY MONDAY TUESDAY WEDNESDAY THURSDAY FRIDAY SATURDAY

Summary

By the end of today, you should be fully aware that the key to managing your boss is to meet their expectations as far as possible. Giving them what they want in terms of communications, updates and outputs is the best way to establish the perfect working relationship – and it is the **psychological** contract that underpins all of this.

You will have discovered by now that establishing the psychological contract is not always straightforward and may involve a bit of detective work as you ask colleagues or rely on observations to enlighten you about your boss's views on, for example, long working hours, frequency of desired updates and levels of preferred proactivity. This information collection phase is often at its most active at the start of new job, but can be started at any point really – it is never too late to start building a psychological contract. And, once you have developed a clear list of expectations and preferred ways of working (for both of you), you can really start to impress your boss – after all, you now know exactly what it takes to impress them!

Tomorrow, then, we look at ways in which you can use your new knowledge to impress your boss.

SUNDAY
MONDAY
TUESDAY
WEDNESDAY
THURSDAY
FRIDAY
SATURDAY

Fact-check (answers at the back)

1. Psychological contracts are...
   a) Written agreements ❏
   b) Legally binding ❏
   c) Informal ❏
   d) Given within 12 weeks of employment commencing ❏

2. Using the phone to communicate is best for...
   a) Discussing complex issues ❏
   b) Telling your boss about your achievements ❏
   c) Issues that need a lot of discussion ❏
   d) Issues requiring an immediate response. ❏

3. Email is *not* useful for...
   a) Queries that don't require an immediate response ❏
   b) Informing your boss of progress ❏
   c) Telling your boss about your achievements ❏
   d) Discussing complex issues ❏

4. Disadvantages of working from home include (tick all that apply)...
   a) Lack of visibility ❏
   b) Missing networking opportunities ❏
   c) It is harder for your boss to manage you ❏
   d) Isolation ❏

5. Reluctant proactivity means that...
   a) Your boss will only allow you to be proactive when your assigned tasks are finished ❏
   b) Your boss expects you to only complete assigned tasks ❏
   c) The boss expects you to generate most of your work projects yourself ❏
   d) Some of your work is assigned and the rest is self-generated. ❏

6. The communications part of the psychological contract should include finding out about (tick all that apply)...
   a) An analysis of your boss's handwriting. ❏
   b) The mode/medium of communication your boss prefers ❏
   c) The frequency of communication ❏
   d) The type of communications you can expect from your boss ❏

7. Modes/media of communication with your boss should rarely include...
   a) Email ❏
   b) Phone ❏
   c) Meetings ❏
   d) Facebook ❏

8. You should keep your boss updated on progress...
a) When they request an update ☐
b) Weekly ☐
c) According to your boss's preferences ☐
d) Daily ☐

9. Working late is...
a) Something I may have to do ☐
b) Something I would never do ☐
c) Something I would ask about when developing my psychological contract ☐
d) Expected ☐

10. In today's climate...
a) I can still expect job security ☐
b) I can still expect my boss to manage my career development ☐
c) I can still expect my boss to allow me to attend relevant training ☐
d) I can expect my boss to identify training opportunities ☐

WEDNESDAY

How to impress your boss

Many people make the mistake of imagining that they should not try too hard to impress their boss out of fear of appearing sycophantic – sucking up too much. But impressing your boss shouldn't be about 'sucking up to them', flattering them or laughing at their jokes – it should be about *impressing* them with your talents, skills and abilities. By now, you should be aware of what makes your boss tick – in other words, what exactly will or will not impress your boss – so today it is a matter of working to meet these expectations. In doing so, you can really start to manage your boss, because the boss who is impressed by you will be more likely to reward you (with, for example, better work projects or promotion). So, in impressing your boss, you are really taking control of your career.

Today, then, we will examine the ways in which you can impress your boss from day one, by creating that all-important brilliant first impression, as well as right through your working life by showing a commitment to professionalism. The role of body language, non-verbal communication and emotion management in creating a great impression are also outlined.

Issues covered today include:

- creating a good first impression
- body language
- emotion management
- professionalism.

Creating a good first impression

First impressions are everything. Humans tend to make snap judgements about people, events and things, simply because we do not have enough time to invest in careful consideration before reaching a decision. And the decision we make as to whether someone or something is good or bad can be long-lasting and difficult to shake off. This means that, if your initial encounter with the boss is negative, you will need to invest a great deal of energy in order to reverse that impression – moreover, everything you do will be tarnished with that negative impression.

On the other hand, a great first impression means that you are blessed with a head start and everything else you do will seem that much better, thanks to that good first impression. Psychologists refer to this as the 'horns or halo effect'. You thus need to make sure the effect you create is a halo (which helps ensure that everything else you do is perceived in a more positive light) rather than horns (which makes everything else you do appear more negative). You can start creating a halo effect from the very first introduction or meeting with your boss. Follow the guidelines in Table 3 below.

Table 3   Guidelines on creating a halo effect at first meeting with boss

| Handshake | Offer a firm handshake with a smile – this conveys self-confidence and interest. Shake your boss's hand no more (or fewer) than three times so as not to create the impression that you are nervous.

Beware about turning your hand down over theirs since this can create an impression of the desire for dominance. Similarly, don't offer an 'overfamiliar' handshake (e.g. involving two hands, grasping your boss's wrist, elbow, shoulder, etc.). |
|---|---|
| Introduction | If appropriate, introduce yourself in a clear, non-apologetic voice. Remember to smile and maintain eye contact. |
| Small talk | Now that the introduction is over, make sure that you don't just stand there looking awkward. Make small talk – comment on the weather (always a good one), your journey there, the building, etc. Try and make a positive rather than negative comment to create the impression that you are upbeat and optimistic. |
| Questions | Ask your boss general questions – nothing too personal or that requires too lengthy or detailed a response. Look interested in their response. |
| Interest | Demonstrate that you are hugely interested in your boss's every word by gazing intently at them (remembering to look away at times too – see later section on body language) and making the occasional affirmative sound such as 'uh-huh'. |
| Dress | See later section on dress codes. |
| Body language | See later section on eye contact and positioning of arms etc. |

Body language

What we say to the boss is sometimes less important than how we say it, and the tone conveyed by our body language can betray our true feelings. On the other hand, being aware of your body language and making it work for you can make the difference between impressing your boss and leaving them with a decidedly negative impression of you. There are two main situations in which you can really use your body language to impress: in meetings and generally in the office. Use the pointers in Table 4 as a guide.

Table 4   Body language in the office

Do...	Don't...
Use 'open' body language such as uncrossed arms and legs. This creates the impression that you have nothing to hide and that you are reasonably confident.	Constantly sit with your legs and arms crossed as this can make you appear secretive and defensive to your boss. It is OK to cross your legs as long as you keep your arms 'open'. Similarly, beware of standing with your hands on your hips or waist in an aggressive stance.
Try and maintain a relaxed stance – even if you have to work at it. It might feel unnatural at first, but try putting one hand in your pocket as you move about, or lean on a desk slightly as you talk to your boss. This conveys confidence.	Hold yourself as if you are a soldier on parade. This can make you seem stiff and formal as well as unsure about yourself – not the impression you want to leave with your boss.
Keep your distance. Personal body space is important, so when you are talking to your boss (or anyone else) make sure you are not too close – if they are constantly edging backwards from you, then you are too close.	Invade your boss's personal space. But neither should you stand too far away either as that can make you seem cold and distant. Try and go by their lead.
Try mirroring your boss's body language. If they incline their head slightly, you do it too. This creates a responsive impression – subtly suggesting that you are in tune with them.	Overdo the mirroring – directly copying every body movement can be downright embarrassing and counterproductive.

Table 5 Body language in meetings

Do...	Don't...
Have a pen in your hand. A pen poised creates the impression that you are ready for action, attentive and interested.	Play with the pen or tap it on the desk as this just creates the impression that you are bored.
Make occasional notes. Again, this really shows you are interested in the proceedings.	Doodle – it will probably be noticed and nothing conveys boredom more!
Sit slightly forward in your chair. This makes you appear to be hanging on to every word and waiting for the right moment to add your own contribution.	Lean back with your hands behind your head. This might be a comfortable position but can make you seem arrogant and overconfident – as if the proceedings of the meeting are somewhat beneath you.
Keep your hands still. Too much flittering and movement conveys the impression that your mind is wandering along with your hands.	Constantly touch your hair or mouth, or pick imaginary bits of fluff off your clothes. This can make you appear, at worse, shifty and, at best, uninterested.

Emotion management

Few people understand what is meant by emotion management, much less use it to impress their boss. Yet it is probably one of the most influential and on-going acts of impression management that you could undertake. Emotion management refers to the deliberate attempt to control the emotions that you present to other people. Most of us perform emotion management at some point in our working (and non-working) lives. For example:

- when we laugh at our boss's (unfunny) joke
- when we express sympathy at our colleague's bad news – even if we don't really care
- when we fake enthusiasm about the achievements of our friend's children
- when we hide our annoyance from that irritating customer.

These are all examples of emotion management – almost unconscious acts that form an important part of all our social interactions. By controlling and managing the emotional front we present to others, we help make interactions run more smoothly, we make people feel good about themselves and we help ensure that the impression we create of ourselves is the one we want others to perceive. Imagine how unpopular we would be if we never engaged in any emotion management! The following three-step guide should help you use emotion management to impress your boss.

Step 1: Recognize the emotions that will impress your boss

Using emotion management to impress your boss is just taking what we all do naturally one step further. The first step is to recognize and acknowledge the emotions that your boss will be impressed by. It is worth noting that research in the area suggests that two kinds of emotional display are best avoided in the workplace. These are:

1 negative emotions such as anger, disappointment, jealousy, etc.
2 extreme displays of emotions (e.g. crying, temper tantrums, inappropriate joy).

So, at the very least, make sure you control your emotions so that you avoid these displays. This means that, even if your boss has really annoyed you, or you have won the lottery (assuming it's not such a big win that you can pack your job in), you should still think carefully about the emotional front you are presenting. Of course, this means that, invariably, you will have to suppress or hide your true feelings at times. Some people feel this is unnecessary and have a kind of 'WYSIWYG' attitude – 'what you see is what you get'. Fair enough, but this won't impress the boss!

So, those are the emotions that won't impress your boss – but which emotions will? Research has shown that most bosses and managers tend to be more impressed by displays of enthusiasm or interest than anything else. Showing enthusiasm demonstrates to your boss that you are keen, hard-working, loyal, that you care about the company, are passionate about your work and are ambitious. All that from a simple act of emotion management!

Of course, it is not just one act of emotion management that is needed – to be truly effective, emotion management needs to be an on-going activity. Display enthusiasm and interest by:

- smiling when you see your boss or when you are assigned tasks or projects
- rising to the challenge of a new piece of work instead of appearing not to want to do it
- being positive about ideas and projects, not negative
- volunteering for jobs
- asking appropriate questions.

You should be careful, however, of two points:

1 Avoid going over the top with your emotional displays. Enthusiasm and interest may well be valued, but constant grinning at your boss every time you see them, boundless enthusiasm for even the most inappropriate tasks and constantly leaping up to volunteer for jobs will not endear you to your colleagues – or your boss. In fact, your boss is more likely to view you as an ingratiating irritant!

2 Avoid reserving your displays of enthusiasm just for your boss's benefit. Switching it on and off like that will make you appear fake rather than enthusiastic and interested. The trick to appearing enthusiastic is to be actually enthusiastic! This way there is nothing false or superficial about you, nor can you be accused of being manipulative. The next step provides tips on creating enthusiasm even when you don't generally feel it.

Step 2: Learn how to 'fake and hide'

It is inevitable that the emotions you ought to display in order to impress your boss will not necessarily be those that you genuinely feel. You will, at times, be obliged to display enthusiasm when you do not feel remotely enthusiastic, or hide anger when you feel it. Consider the following scenarios:

- You are preoccupied by a personal worry or concern
- You are distressed by an argument with your partner
- You have a health worry
- You have been passed over for promotion
- Your colleague is assigned a task that should have gone to you
- A customer is winding you up
- Your boss wants your opinion on a project that doesn't interest you
- Your car broke down and you are late for a meeting
- A customer has just been rude to you
- You feel unwell.

These are common situations that occur on a day-to-day basis at work that may make it very difficult for you to display the required emotions – while simultaneously hiding your real ones. Yet, if you are to impress and, ultimately, manage, your boss, fake and hide you must. There are two approaches to this emotional acting and both have their roots in schools of professional acting:

- **Surface acting:** Professional actors know this as 'technical' acting and it involves simply arranging your physical features so that they reflect the emotion you want to display. That is, in this approach, there is no need to try and feel the required emotion at all. However, the act of arranging your facial features in, for example, a smile could in itself induce the associated feeling of cheer because it is thought that the very act of smiling causes physiological and chemical changes in our brain – making us feel happy.
- **Deep acting:** This is known by professional actors as the 'method' approach and involves the actor attempting to conjure up the emotion that they are required to display. In other words, in this approach you would actually try to feel enthusiastic. The founder of method acting, Stanislavski, advises that this can be achieved by using a technique called 'emotional memory' which involves you recalling an experience or incident when you did feel the required emotion in the past – and using that memory to help you feel that emotion now.

Both these approaches are fine if it is the occasional bit of acting that you must do. For instance, my research has shown that most of us hide or fake emotion in about a third of our workplace communications and doing so allows us to impress the boss so that we can get ahead at work. However, if you find that you are hiding and faking emotion constantly, then it is time for a reassessment.

Perhaps you never feel enthusiastic about work, or dislike your boss. It is difficult under those circumstances to manage your boss without addressing the root cause of your work-based dissatisfaction. The 'common problems' covered on Saturday might help.

Step 3: Diagnosing the emotional culture at work

In addition to ensuring that you display emotions such as enthusiasm and interest in Steps 1 and 2, the good emotion and impression manager will go one step further if they really want to manage their boss. They will diagnose the emotional culture of their organization so that they can be sure that their own emotional demeanour matches. The emotional culture of the organization refers to the unwritten rules about which emotions are expected to be displayed and which ought to be hidden – these are not the same for every organization or industry. More creative industries allow freer emotional expression and it may even be appropriate in some to display the extreme emotional displays so frowned upon in other office cultures. On the other hand, some emotional cultures are such that no emotions are expected at all – not even enthusiasm. For more on emotion management, see my book *Hiding What We Feel, Faking What We Don't* (Element).

Professionalism

What does it mean to be professional? Being professional is the difference between doing your job adequately and doing it well enough to justify not only your salary, but a possible increase, too. Professionalism is about attention to detail, showing you care about your work and not letting anyone (including yourself) down. Professionalism is about proving to your boss that you are more than capable and this is why it is a key aspect of managing your boss – if your boss trusts you and relies on you, they will be more likely to reward you with extra responsibilities, perks, training, etc. Achieve professionalism by careful attention to the following areas.

Personal appearance

In general, you should aim to ensure that your personal appearance sets you apart from a student on work placement. This means neat hair, ironed clothes and an emphasis on classic rather than trendy clothes. Go easy on fussy details such as jewellery and overpowering scents. The impression you should be trying to create is that you are hard-working and not preoccupied or distracted by your appearance. In addition, you want your boss to be confident that you are presentable to clients and customers – even if such people should arrive unexpectedly.

Of course, what you wear depends on the dress code of your office and, like the emotional culture discussed above, this can vary between industries and organizations. It might be more acceptable in creative industries such as music or the media to wear casual attire, but less so in most other industries. The best way of ensuring you look as professional as you can be is to dress in a similar style as your boss – dress for the job you want, not the job you have.

Time management

Perfecting your time management skills is a vital step to appearing professional. If you have good time management skills, you should have few problems in:

● submitting reports on time
● meeting deadlines

- being able to update your boss on progress whenever it is requested
- being punctual at meetings
- arriving on time at work
- being able to give accurate estimates as to how long work projects will take you.

All these are signs of professionalism. Improve your time management skills by:

- learning to prioritize work so that you complete the most urgent or important tasks first rather than the ones you want to do first
- delegating where possible
- discouraging interruptions – a huge amount of time is wasted through interruptions from colleagues and phone calls. If you are completing a task for a deadline, either build interruption time into your estimate of how long it will take you, or put your voicemail on and a 'please do not disturb' sign on your office door
- being organized in terms of your filing and storage systems
- keeping checklists so that you know exactly what needs doing and you don't end up forgetting anything
- being realistic so that when you estimate how long a job will take, you do not underestimate. Similarly, make sure you do not take on tasks that you will not have time to complete.

Your desk

Your desk can make or break your impression as a professional. Create a professional image by:

- keeping your desk clutter-free
- having an in-tray system that shows a good volume of 'out' work completed
- keeping personal possessions such as photographs to a minimum
- choosing decorative items with care – pot plants are fine, but avoid silly computer mats or novelty pens.

Presentation of work

The appearance of your work is an indicator of your professionalism. It is not enough for it just to be delivered on time or even to be of superior quality – it must look professional, too. This allows the way your work is presented to act as a 'halo' so that the good impression created is seen in the content, too (see earlier notes on the halo effect). Create a professional image in your work by:

- ensuring accuracy – check and double-check
- avoiding spelling, grammatical and typing errors
- binding reports in suitable covers
- using colour in reports or presentations appropriately.

Summary

By the end of today you will have learned that creating a great impression starts with being body-language aware. Handshakes, small talk, dress and posture have all been discussed, so you should know how to create the right impression in the office and in meetings. Hand in hand with body language is emotion management and today we have seen how controlling and managing the emotional front we present to others at work can really help improve our relationship with the boss and others. By following the three steps outlined today, emotion management can be an integral part of all your work relationships.

Part of the skills discussed today includes social acting skills and there has to be a recognition that impression management can sometimes involve surface or deep acting. However, to create a really great impression, we have seen that acting the part is not enough – being a true professional at work is what really counts. Being professional can mean different things within different workplaces but at the very least should include consideration of time management, appropriate personal appearance and excellent presentation of your work. By incorporating all these elements into your work life, you should ensure that you create a very positive impression on your boss – even if, on occasion, you are having to fake it a bit!

SUNDAY
MONDAY
TUESDAY
WEDNESDAY
THURSDAY
FRIDAY
SATURDAY

Fact-check (answers at the back)

1. The halo or horns effect refers to...
   a) The lasting effect of the positive or negative first impression that you make ❏
   b) The effect that the firmness of your handshake makes ❏
   c) Whether you smile or frown when you met someone ❏
   d) The positive or negative language that you use ❏

2. A good handshake should...
   a) Involve at least three shakes of the hand ❏
   b) Involve you turning your hand down over the other person's ❏
   c) Include both your hands ❏
   d) Should be firm, brief and accompanied with a smile ❏

3. In the office, it is good to...
   a) Always sit with arms and legs crossed ❏
   b) Stand with your hands on your hips ❏
   c) Try to have 'open' body language ❏
   d) Copy your boss's every body movement ❏

4. In meetings, create a good impression by...
   a) Holding a pen in your hand
   b) Doodling ❏
   c) Leaning back with your hands behind your head ❏
   d) Tap your fingers on the desk ❏

5. Generally, which of the following emotions should you avoid displaying at work?
   a) Interest ❏
   b) Anger ❏
   c) Enthusiasm ❏
   d) Pleasure ❏

6. How should you *not* display enthusiasm and interest?
   a) Smiling ❏
   b) Being positive about ideas and projects ❏
   c) Volunteering for jobs ❏
   d) Telling jokes ❏

7. How should you *not* fake emotions at work?
   a) Arranging your face into the appropriate features ❏
   b) Thinking of something that would make you feel the required emotion ❏
   c) Remembering a situation where you felt the emotion you are required to feel ❏
   d) Pretending to feel the emotion ❏

8. Being professional mean...
   a) Doing your job adequately ❏
   b) Cutting corners when necessary ❏
   c) Paying attention to detail ❏
   d) Pretending to care about your work ❏

9. Good time-management skills mean that you should...
a) Submit work on time ❑
b) Be punctual at meetings ❑
c) Be able to estimate how long a job will take ❑
d) Do as much as you can yourself and not rely on other people ❑

10. Create a good 'desk' impression by...
a) Having plenty of clutter to show how busy you are ❑
b) Keep personal possessions on display to a minimum ❑
c) Have lots of fun items on display ❑
d) Have an overflowing in-tray to show how much work you have to do ❑

THURSDAY

Getting more from your boss

Today is about discovering how to get more from your boss. You should be well on your way to managing your boss now, but this is about more than just getting along. Effective boss management means that you will be able to ask for – and get – more, because, let's face it, by now you will have certainly proved your worth.

Many employees find it very difficult to tell their boss that they are not happy with the status quo, whether that be with regards to pay, promotion or workload – with the consequence that they end up lumbered with too much work, boring tasks, dull jobs, poor pay or are overlooked for promotion for too long. But, hopefully by now, you will have the confidence in your abilities to impress your boss and will feel able to push the boundaries a little more.

The main reason that we often feel unsure about asking for more at work is because we are unassertive and unaware of our basic rights at work, so we will start today by examining these issues. Once we have established these basics, we can discuss ways of asking for a rise, asking for promotion, requesting more challenging work, and trying to get your workload reduced.

Today, then, will focus on approaching some of the more common areas that need to be addressed in order to get more from your boss. These include:

- asking for a rise
- seeking promotion
- requesting more challenging work
- dealing with work overload.

Why do we accept the way things are at work?

Before tackling these issues, it is worth addressing the question of why so many people feel unable to ask for what they want from their boss. Common reasons for people accepting rather than challenging the status quo include:

- 'I don't want to rock the boat.'
- 'I don't want my boss to think that I am not dedicated enough by complaining about my work hours.'
- 'My boss likes enthusiastic workers – I will seem like a moaner if I complain.'
- 'I should be able to cope, shouldn't I? If I ask for a reduction in my workload, I will seem less capable.'
- 'I can't ask for a rise because, if my boss hasn't already given me one, maybe he doesn't think I deserve it.'
- 'Maybe I am not good enough for promotion.'

All these statements and sentiments reflect a lack of self-confidence and a failure to recognize basic work rights. The trick, then, to getting more from your boss is to become more assertive at work.

Becoming more assertive at work

The first step to becoming more assertive is to recognize and accept the work-related rights that you, as an employee, have. These include:

- the right to be fairly paid for the work you do
- the right to perform tasks for which you are qualified to do – and not to perform tasks for which you are not qualified
- the right to enjoy a life outside work
- the right to equality of opportunity
- the right not to be threatened, abused or otherwise harassed at work
- the right to say no to inappropriate requests at work
- the right to work under conditions that are not detrimental to your physical or mental health.

In addition to these basic 'moral' rights, every employee also has legal rights. These include:

- the right not to be dismissed unfairly
- the right to return after maternity leave
- the right not to be discriminated against because of disability, sex or race
- the right to have time off for antenatal care
- the right to (unpaid) time off for public duties (such as jury duty) and for trade union activities
- the right to time off in the event of redundancy to look for work or arrange training
- the right to a written statement of reason for dismissal
- the right to have itemized pay statements
- the right not to have employment contract breached
- the right to be paid the national minimum wage.

Sources: Advisory, Conciliation and Arbitration Service (Acas) and Department of Trade and Industry (UK).

If you are able to accept that you have these rights (as do all your colleagues, and, indeed, your boss), then you are halfway to being able to assert them. Much of the reticence that workers have in asking for more from their boss is tied up with their being unsure of these basic rights that they have. Thus, if you can accept that you have the right to a life outside work, for instance, then it is easier to give yourself 'permission' to complain about being expected to work weekends. Similarly, if you believe that you are entitled to work under conditions that are not going to have pernicious effects on your health, you should feel more comfortable about challenging a work environment that is particularly stressful.

Of course, it's one thing to realize that it is perfectly acceptable to ask your boss for more, but it's quite another actually doing it! The remainder of today's section will help.

Asking for a rise

Before you even think about how to go about asking for a rise, stop and ask yourself one crucial question: do I deserve a rise? That might seem like a strange question, but many people make the mistake of seeking a rise for the wrong reasons. Such reasons include:

- 'My colleague has got a rise so I should, too.'
- 'I have been with the firm a long time.'
- 'My friend who works for company X earns more than me.'
- 'I have just had a baby – I need more money.'

None of these reasons are anything to do with the value you offer the company and thus are irrelevant when it comes to seeking a rise. Legitimate reasons (over and above normal inflationary increases) include:

- 'I have been given more responsibility at work and thus should be paid accordingly.'
- 'I am working longer hours because there is more work to do (not because I am a slow worker).'
- 'I have saved the company money (e.g. with a cost-cutting idea).'
- 'I am expected to work more unsociable hours.'
- 'I am expected to travel or be away from home more.'
- 'I have gained relevant new skills or qualifications which mean I am adding more value.'

Once you have established that you have a good case, your next task is figuring out how to manage your boss so that they agree! The best strategy is to present a logical, coherent argument and present it either as a written 'report' or verbal 'presentation'. Either way, you will need to arrange a meeting with your boss. If there is an appraisal system in place in your company, a good time to do this is at that point. (If there is no appraisal scheme, you might like to suggest one for yourself – it is just an annual review of your strengths and weaknesses so that training needs, promotion prospects, etc. can be identified.) When you meet with your boss, using the following pointers as guidelines should help you have a successful outcome:

- **Don't threaten.** It is common for workers to make the mistake of saying things such as: 'If I don't get a pay rise, I will be forced to look for alternative employment.' Don't make such threats unless you fully intend to follow them through (and only if you actually have a job to go to!). Many bosses will be irritated by such threats and may well take you up on your offer.
- **Don't demand.** You have every right to *request* a pay rise, but you cannot *demand* one. Nothing will annoy your boss more than a feeling that their hand is being forced.
- **Stay calm.** It is normal to feel quite emotional about the request – after all, it is your livelihood at stake. Staying calm and reasonable will help; becoming petulant or emotional will not. Of course, there is still every possibility that the boss may say 'no', however well reasoned your argument might be. It could be that your boss does not think you deserve one after all, or that they simply cannot afford any more money. In the former case, it is worth finding out what more you could do to become more deserving. In the latter case, ask for a review in, say, six months' time. In both cases, this should ensure that 'no' is not the final answer.

Another common excuse that some bosses give for turning down a request for a rise is that 'If I give you one I will have to give one to your colleagues.' This is an unacceptable reason and you will have to make it clear that you are representing yourself only and that you do not and will not discuss your salary with anyone else.

Seeking promotion

Many of the issues regarding seeking promotion are similar to those concerned with asking for a pay rise. However, seeking promotion involves some extra considerations. There are two main scenarios:

1 There is a specific vacancy that you wish to be promoted to.
2 There is no specific vacancy – you just want to move up the grading scale.

Both these scenarios require different approaches to the boss. Where there is a specific vacancy – for instance when a more senior person has left the firm leaving their position vacant – you will have to persuade your boss not only that you are suitable for the higher-graded post, but that you are more suitable than anyone else. It is increasingly common for any vacancy to be advertised externally, so you may be competing against an unknown entity, too.

The first step is to approach your boss to 'stake your claim'. Follow these guidelines:

● As soon as the vacancy becomes apparent (this could be before the other person has left), meet with your boss and explain why you think you would be the best person for the job.
● Include in your argument any evidence to show that you could do the job well and remember to point out why you want the job so much.
● Whatever you do, avoid criticizing the previous incumbent of the post! If you have some ideas on changes or improvements you would make, present them is a way that does not appear critical of your hoped-for predecessor.

At this point, it is likely that you will receive some feedback regarding your application. Hopefully it will be of the positive 'go-for-it' kind! You may be invited or advised to submit a written application or to apply along the same route as everyone else. Because this is the likely outcome, some people make the mistake of bypassing the boss completely and jump straight to the application stage. Since your boss is sure to be asked about your suitability, it is eminently sensible to gain their approval first – they are far more likely to recommend you if they have been consulted in advance.

But, what if the feedback from your boss is less than positive? Find out the reason – then you can do something about it if necessary. Perhaps your boss does not think you are ready for the responsibility or thinks you lack some necessary skill or experience. Whatever it is that they think is missing from your portfolio, now is your chance to ask for the training or tasks that will fill the gap. If you consider your boss's assessment of you to be fair, it is wise not to go ahead with the application for promotion.

However, suppose you consider your boss's comments to be unfair or untrue? Suppose they claim that you have not demonstrated managerial skills – yet you know you ran the office effectively for one month while your superior was off sick? The trick here is to tactfully point this out – without actually appearing to say to your boss, 'You are SO wrong!' Ask whether they are aware of the positive feedback you received while managing the office for that month and explain how much you enjoyed the challenge and that you feel ready for more. If you are totally unable to convince your boss, it might be worth trying to convince someone else from a different company – i.e. look for another job at the level you want. However, you should bear in mind that your current boss is likely to be asked for a reference.

So why might your boss refuse to refer you for promotion, even when you seem to have the right skills and experience? Of course, it is always possible that they are right and you are overplaying your abilities. On the other hand, there are rare circumstances when a boss might deliberately hold you back, either because they don't want to lose you or because they feel threatened by you. Both these scenarios are difficult to overcome and, if you suspect this is happening to you, it really could be time to jump ship (see if there is anyone else in the firm who could give you a reference).

When there is no specific vacancy, much of the above will still apply, except you are in a slightly better position in that you don't have to wait for someone else to leave! A good time to suggest a grading promotion is at your annual review or when you have just gained some relevant skill or qualification. Again, if the answer is 'no', find out what you will need to do to get a 'yes' next time. And make sure you do it!

Requesting more challenging work

Many people remain stuck with entry-level tasks for years simply because they are waiting for their boss to give them more rewarding work. Don't wait! Asking for more challenging work demonstrates enthusiasm and keenness – and most bosses like that! The best advice here, then, is to be proactive and always be on the lookout for more interesting tasks that you could offer to do. Suggest pieces of work that you could take on – either tasks that would save your boss from doing them, ideas that you have come up with, or those bits of work that no one else in the office wants. Here are a few top tips:

- To show your ability, actually do something (even if it is only a mock-up) and show it to your boss.
- If you want to learn a new skill that will help you get more rewarding work, shadow or watch a more experienced colleague.
- Request training so that you will be able to take on more interesting work.
- Spend time with the people whose jobs you aspire to – you can learn plenty from them over informal chats at lunch.
- Always ask to do specific pieces of work – don't just vaguely complain that the work is not 'challenging enough'.
- Be realistic – don't run before you can walk. There is no point asking to edit a newsletter, for instance, if you have never written a feature for it.

Dealing with work overload

Many readers may have turned to this section first, since having too much work to do is a very common problem. But what is 'too much'? You know you are suffering from work overload if:

- you are continually having to work late
- you have to take work home with you
- you always feel pressured and stressed
- you never have time for lunch.

Work overload is potentially quite a serious issue, as it is a significant source of stress in the workplace. And stress itself can lead to a lowered immunity, which is why you are likely to suffer from repeated colds, flu and other ailments. Remember your rights, and take action. Arrange a meeting with your boss and present them with a time sheet in which you have listed your work tasks and time taken over the past month.

This should demonstrate clearly that you have too much work. Explain that you are happy for occasional heavy workloads – e.g. when deadlines are approaching or a heavy order needs completing – but that you cannot continue like this indefinitely. If you can suggest solutions to the problem, then all the better since it will always impress if you appear to have the firm's interests at heart as well as your own. For instance, there may be areas of your job that could be cut out or delegated to someone else. There may be some tasks that could be compromised on in terms of cutting corners. Of course, it may be that there simply needs to be more staff – not usually a welcome suggestion in these cost-cutting days!

The final word of this section has to be – don't put up with chronic work overload. Your health could well suffer, so if your boss is not forthcoming with help, then think about moving on.

Summary

By the end of today, you will have learned how to get more from your boss in four main areas – asking for a pay rise or promotion, requesting more challenging work and reducing your workload. All of these rely on your being aware of what you are entitled to at work and in giving yourself 'permission' to stand up for your rights if they are not being respected. It is sometimes easier for us to not 'rock the boat' by asking for more, but it is important for our self-respect, and to earn respect from the boss, to make a stand when it is appropriate to do so.

All of this, then, relies on knowing our worth and thus having good reason for asking for a rise or promotion. Having legitimate reasons is the first step, and by the end of today you should be able to implement strategies to approach your boss with your request (remembering to never threaten to leave if you don't mean it!). Of course, even with all the techniques learned today, sometimes you will just have an unreasonable boss and your best efforts will go unrewarded; tomorrow, then, we start looking at coping with this situation – when you have the boss from hell!

SUNDAY

MONDAY

TUESDAY

WEDNESDAY

THURSDAY

FRIDAY

SATURDAY

Fact-check (answers at the back)

1. Which of the following do you have the right to at work?
   a) The right to finish at 5 p.m. every day ❑
   b) The right to never work weekends ❑
   c) The right to have nice colleagues ❑
   d) The right to enjoy a life outside work ❑

2. My legal rights at work do *not* include...
   a) The right to receive the minimum wage ❑
   b) The right not to have my employment contract breached ❑
   c) The right to have paid time off work for trade union activities ❑
   d) The right not to be dismissed unfairly ❑

3. A good reason to ask for a rise is...
   a) My colleague has got a rise so I should too ❑
   b) I have been with this firm for a long time now ❑
   c) I have more responsibility at work now ❑
   d) I need more money now I have a family ❑

4. When asking for a rise I should...
   a) Make it clear that, if I don't get what I want, I will look for employment elsewhere. ❑
   b) Stay calm ❑
   c) Try to force my boss into admitting I deserve a rise ❑
   d) Show how angry I will be if I don't get the rise I deserve ❑

5. When a vacancy arises for promotion, I should...
   a) Explain to my boss why I would be the best person for the job ❑
   b) Explain why I will be so much better than the previous incumbent of the post ❑
   c) Be modest about my abilities – it doesn't do to show off ❑
   d) Not bother discussing it with my boss – just get an application in ❑

6. If I want more challenging work I should...
   a) Wait patiently for my boss to give me better work ❑
   b) Complain to my boss that the work isn't challenging enough ❑
   c) Request or attend training to improve my skills ❑
   d) Tell everyone how over-skilled I am for my current work ❑

7. Which of the following would *not* suggest that you are suffering from work overload?
a) You are bored at work ❑
b) You are always having to work late or take work home with me ❑
c) You never have time for lunch ❑
d) You always feel stressed and pressured ❑

8. Work overload is potentially serious because...
a) It is a significant source of workplace stress ❑
b) You end up missing your train home ❑
c) It stops you using your skills ❑
d) It stops you getting promotion ❑

9. A good reason for *not* complaining about workload is...
a) It is only at certain times of the year that we are exceptionally busy ❑
b) I don't want my boss to think that I am not dedicated enough ❑
c) I will seem less enthusiastic if I complain ❑
d) My boss will think I can't cope ❑

10. Which of these is *not* a good reason to try to get more from your boss?
a) It will help me get ahead ❑
b) It will be good for my career ❑
c) They will respect me more ❑
d) I have the right to more ❑

FRIDAY

Dealing with the boss from hell

By this stage, you should have plenty of tools in your skills toolbox to enable you to get the most from your boss – to impress them and to work in the way that best meets their expectations and needs. However, all of the skills you have learned do rely on you having a boss who is a fairly reasonable and rational human being who wants to establish a good working relationship with you just as much as you want to establish one with them.

However, what do you do if you don't have a reasonable boss? How can you manage the boss when they are the boss from hell? Perhaps your boss is unwilling to listen to reason, is motivated by selfish desires, suffers from an inferiority complex, has a major chip on their shoulder, is arrogant or is even a bully. Such a boss is unlikely to respond to the sort of techniques that have been outlined thus far, such as through the psychological contract (Tuesday) or impression management (Wednesday).

If you are unfortunate enough to have the boss from hell, you may well need to take more dramatic action. So today we will discuss how to deal with the three worst types of bosses from hell:

- the bullying boss
- the sexually harassing boss
- the glory-stealing boss.

Is your boss a bully?

Before we talk about how to deal with the boss who is bullying you, we need to define what we mean by a bullying boss. When does a bad-tempered, rude boss, become a bully? One researcher, Andrea Adams (1992), defined such bullying as 'persistent criticism and personal abuse, both in public and in private, which humiliates and demeans the individual, gradually eroding their sense of self', while the Manufacturing, Science and Finance Trade Union (MSF) in the UK states that bullying at work is 'persistent, offensive, abusive, intimidating, malicious or insulting behaviour, abuse of power or unfair penal sanctions, which makes the recipient feel upset, threatened, humiliated or vulnerable, which undermines their self-confidence and which may cause them to suffer stress' (*IDS Employment Law Supplement* No. 76, 1996). As a general guide, your boss may be a bully if they:

- explode angrily – either in an indiscriminate way or in a focused manner
- pick on you (or/and others) unfairly
- humiliate you in front of others
- pressure you into doing things you don't want to do or doing things their way

- force you to abandon your own plans (e.g. by making you work late against your will)
- have power over you – they can fire you if you don't do what they want
- constantly criticize you
- ridicule you
- belittle your achievements
- unreasonably refuse your requests
- set unrealistic deadlines
- shout at you (or others).

Care should be taken when trying to decide if your boss could be classed as a bully. They do not need to display all of these behaviours, but the point is that their behaviour is continually abusive rather than a one-off. Your boss is not a bully if their complaints about you are focused and justified.

Is it serious?

If you do indeed think that your boss might be a bully, then, yes, it is a very serious matter. Some people have the view that bullying bosses are par for the course – a result of the everyday pressures and strains of work. Bosses, they argue, do not have time for common niceties – they must shout and cajole to get things done. But there is a clear difference between an impatient or stressed boss and the bullying one. You will probably know if your boss is a bully without having to go through the checklist above. Research shows that workplace bullying can lead to serious health problems and you may already be experiencing one or more of the following:

- feelings of high stress
- repeated colds and minor infections
- depression or other mental health problems
- inability to perform your job
- dread of work.

In fact, workplace bullying is now taken very seriously. It has long been recognized as 'a significant factor contributing to workplace stress, with potentially substantial costs for both

individuals and for industry' (IRS Employment Trends 1992: 2).
According to a British survey in 1997 by Charlotte Raynor at
Staffordshire University, a quarter of adult workers have been
subjected to bullying at some point in their working lives while
another study suggests that some 40 million working days are
thought to be lost each year in Britain alone due to the effects
of bullying in the workplace (Le Poidewin 1996).

Why is your boss a bully?

Psychologists and researchers have invested a great deal of
energy into trying to find out why people bully. Several theories
have emerged, including:

The childhood pay-off theory

Randall (1997) said that to understand why adults bully,
'it is first necessary to understand that most of them have
discovered in childhood that bullying has positive pay-offs'
(p. 22). For some, bullying may be a way of attempting to come
to terms with abuse suffered as a child (Crawford in Adams
1992b). For others, their behaviour may be an attempt to win
love or attention from their parents, reflecting parental neglect.
This bully, then, is likely to be a bully even if they were not a
boss – they do not use bullying as a means of managing, but as
a general means to get what they want.

The envy/threat theory

Others argue that envy is a major motivator for bullying
behaviour. Thus, a bully boss may 'attack certain individuals
for a variety of reasons, the most prevalent being the victim's
popularity among colleagues, their success, achievement,
efficiency, organizational expertise and superior social skills'
(Alexandrou 1995: 30).

This boss feels threatened by the up-and-coming
subordinate who may seem to be better at the job than they
are and may eventually usurp them. This boss is insecure and
lacks confidence in their own abilities and is more likely to
bully just one or two people than a larger group.

The personality theory

Many researchers argue that bullies have certain personality or behavioural characteristics. For instance, according to Rayner and Cooper (1997), there are four types of bully-boss, ranging from the pathological bully who bullies for enjoyment, the situational bully who resorts to bullying when under pressure, the role-playing bully who feels that bullying behaviour is expected of him and the punishing bully who believes that punishment is an effective means of management. As Raynor and Cooper (1997) state, 'many people bully because they have staff whom they find difficult and do not know how else to manage them, some people bully as a means of passing on their own stress, others bully because they work in environments where this is the norm and they can simply get away with it' (1997: 214).

Managing the bully-boss

There are a range of strategies that the victim of a bully-boss can adopt. These include:

Knowing your rights

Yesterday we looked at workers' rights, and it is important to revisit and remember these if your boss is a bully.

Often, bullying behaviour will infringe upon these rights. In addition to the rights that every worker is entitled to, there are legal rights that are relevant to the bully-boss. Although you have no legal right not to be bullied at work, if your boss's bullying causes you to leave your job, become ill or is based on sexual or racial harassment (see next section), then you may have a case to take legal action. In addition, the Criminal Justice and Public Order Act 1994 created a criminal offence of 'intentional harassment' which could apply to the bully-boss if they threaten or insult you. There is also the Protection from Harassment Act of 1997, which could be applied, although it is more commonly used to stop stalkers. The Human Rights Act 1998 may well be another weapon against the bully-boss if such behaviour means that the worker's rights to be treated humanely are violated. You will need to take legal advice in order to implement any of these acts, but this should be considered only if all else has failed.

Confrontation

Knowing your rights is one thing, but being able to assert them is something else. Being assertive with a bully-boss means calmly pointing out that you dislike their behaviour and find it unacceptable – in other words, you have to confront your boss. The best way to confront a bully-boss is probably not in a reactive way – that is, not when he or she has just bullied you. Such a confrontation is likely to be aggressive (either on your or the bully's part) and counterproductive. To confront your bully-boss effectively, you need to arrange a meeting with them and explain your concerns. Explain that you feel victimized, or that you feel pressured to do things or that your rights are infringed. Be polite and calm – but not apologetic. You could even ask why the bully is behaving like this – it is always possible that your boss has no idea about the distress they are causing (especially if they feel that bullying is a normal and effective management tool). If confrontation fails, you may need to try the next strategy.

Making an official complaint

To do this, you will need to amass evidence of your bully-boss's behaviour. Keep a diary of any incidents that cause you distress. Note what happened and when. Mention any witnesses to the incident as well as how it made you feel. Now you are ready to complain.

The first thing to do is to find out if your company has a policy regarding workplace bullying. Some do, although this is not yet a legal requirement (unlike schools, which are legally required to have an anti-bullying policy). If there is a policy, you can follow the guidelines in that. Otherwise, you will have to follow a formal grievances procedure (ask your personnel department if you are not sure about this). If your firm is a smaller one without such procedures, then make a complaint in writing to your boss's line manager or superior. Within the letter, explain that you have evidence and witnesses and that you would like action taken. If a formal complaint does not halt the bully-boss in their tracks, you may have to consider taking legal action.

Taking legal action

This should always be considered a last resort since it is costly and time-consuming and usually means that you will have to leave your job in order to have a case (such as for constructive dismissal). By this stage, you should have amassed a good portfolio of evidence and probably medical evidence, too – visits to your doctor with stress-related problems can be used as evidence. Approach your Citizens Advice Bureau, trade union, Acas or a solicitor for advice on how to proceed (see, too, the next section on sexual harassment).

The sexually harassing boss

Sexual harassment occurs when your boss (or any other person, of course) offers: 'unwanted conduct affecting the dignity of men and women in the workplace... The key is that the actions or comments are viewed as demeaning and unacceptable to the recipient' (Acas, bullying and harassment at work booklet, July 1999). Harassment (which can be by male or female bosses towards male or female subordinates) can be an isolated incident but is usually persistent. Generally, sexual harassment could involve:

● unwelcome sexual advances such as touching
● standing too close
● sexual comments
● display of offensive materials
● questions of a sexual nature
● personal comments regarding physical attributes.

Your boss does not need to do any of this face-to-face – sexual harassment can also occur within written communications, including email and texts, or by phone. Is it serious? Like bullying, sexual harassment can have serious effects on the health and wellbeing of employees. Victims may feel:

- anxious
- unable to cope
- humiliated
- unwilling to go to work
- frightened
- demotivated
- angry
- unwell
- frustrated
- stressed.

All these commonly experienced symptoms can, of course, lead to reduced work performance, absence from work and even resignation. Employers do have a legal responsibility to protect your health, safety and welfare (in the UK under the Health and Safety and Work Act, 1974). However, if it is your boss doing the harassment, what can you do? Use the following plan as a guide.

Confrontation

The first step is to let your boss know that their actions are causing you distress. They genuinely may not mean to harass you and may think they are just being flirty or fun. Some people are more 'touchy-feely' than others and may not realize how offensive their behaviour is. By telling your boss, you are giving them a chance to stop, which they will do if it was unintended. Even if they are aware that their behaviour is inappropriate, by confronting them, they can see that you are aware of your rights and will not accept their behaviour – in many cases this is enough to stop them. Be firm, not aggressive, and be positive and calm (but not apologetic). The following, for example, would be a reasonable approach: 'You might not realize but when you put your arm around me in the office / tell smutty jokes, I feel very uncomfortable and I would like you to stop doing this.' If you find it too difficult to confront your boss face-to-face, try sending an email or memo (keep a copy and any reply).

Keep a diary

As with the bullying boss, you are advised to make a note of any incidents that you feel are evidence that your boss is sexually harassing you. Record the date, times, any witnesses, and how you felt and so on. Keep copies of any relevant evidence such as letters, memos, tapes, emails, etc. Keep records of any medical help you seek (such as treatment for stress or depression).

Seek advice

Talk to your union, Citizens Advice or an Acas public enquiry point. Any of these sources may be able to advise you on how to proceed and what action to take – and whether or not you have a case for legal action.

Formal complaint

This procedure would be similar to that when dealing with the bully-boss (see above).

Employment tribunal

Like the bullying situation, you will usually only be able to assert your legal rights if you leave the organization (although claims alleging sex discrimination can be made while you are still employed). If you do take legal action, it will probably involve going to an employment tribunal and the tribunal will expect you to have made every effort to resolve the problem yourself first. There is usually a three-month period from the time you leave your job (or the infringement of your rights) during which you can bring a complaint to a tribunal. An employee wishing to make a complaint can obtain an application form from an Employment Service Jobcentre (also downloadable from www.direct.gov.uk/en/Diol1/DoItOnline/DG_4017934). Before a full hearing takes place, attempts at conciliation will be made.

The glory-stealing boss

The glory-stealing boss is the one who:

- passes off your ideas as their own
- criticizes your ideas but rejigs them as their own
- claims responsibility for your successes – although not your failures
- does not give you credit for good work.

Such a boss may not seem quite as 'hellish' as the bullying or harassing boss and, certainly, there are unlikely to be avenues of legal redress to turn to. But the glory-stealing boss can still make your work life very difficult and can even block promotions and career progression. After all, if no one knows how well you are doing, how will you ever get promoted? And, when it comes to redundancies, you could be first in line if your skills and talent are not filtering out beyond your department through to the powers-that-be.

A good boss will always credit you with good work – and tell others about you. After all, it reflects well on them if their staff are performing well. However, to an insecure boss, the fear is that you will outperform them – which is why they may feel the need to claim the credit and keep you in your place.

Is your boss stealing your glory?

It can take a while before you find out that your glory is being stolen – especially if your boss creates the impression that they have been singing your praises to all and sundry. It might be several months (or even years) down the line before you find out that your boss never mentions you at those board meetings. So, the first step to dealing with this kind of boss from hell is to find out if there is a problem at all. Here are the clues you should be looking out for:

- Ideas that your boss has said will 'never work' later appear in memos or reports that they have produced.
- Your boss encourages you to put their name as co-author of any report you prepare.
- When you speak to people from other departments they know nothing of your successes.
- When you meet senior management they barely seem to know who you are.
- Your boss insists that personal glory detracts from team effort – and thus your name is left out of reports detailing the 'department's' successes.
- Your boss encourages all upward communications to go through them.

Beating the glory-stealing boss

The glory-stealing boss can be beaten, but it takes some effort. Once you are fairly sure that your boss is either stealing your credit or blocking your glory from reaching beyond the department, it is time to take action. The next time you have a major success (a great idea, a money-saving strategy, etc.), follow this boss-management plan:

Keep records

Keep records of any memos or conversations you have with your boss so that you can prove that those great ideas have indeed been initiated by yourself – and not by your boss. Keep copies of replies from your boss – and encourage written ones by emailing or memoing queries (such as 'Have you had a chance to look over my idea yet?') rather than face-to-face or on the phone.

Get the evidence

It is always a good idea to obtain some piece of external evidence to back up your brilliance, otherwise it is easy for your boss to belittle your achievement. Evidence can include a letter from a customer, statistical reports documenting savings, an original (dated) memo outlining a proposal, and so on.

Bypass your boss

There's no easy way round this – your boss cannot be trusted to spread the word so you will need to do it yourself. Your method of (self-)publicity depends on what it is you want to tell the world about. A memo to head office or to the executive board might be best if there is something really outstanding to report – but remember to mention your boss in a positive way to deflect the inevitable unfavourable response from them to your actions. They will be less likely to berate you for going above them if your memo was full of praise regarding the encouragement they gave you. Alternatively, simply make sure that you 'bump' into your boss's boss – and casually mention your achievement to them!

Summary

Today we have dealt with three of the worse types of boss from hell. The bully-boss is probably the most common of these and, if you are unfortunate to have such a boss, it is important that you recognize the problem and learn to manage this very difficult situation.

As we have seen today, there is a range of strategies that you can adopt including knowing your rights, confronting the bully, making an official complaint and, finally, the prospect of taking legal action. Similar strategies can be used with a boss who sexually harasses you. In both cases, keeping diaries of all incidents is a vital first step.

The glory-stealing boss can be just as difficult to deal with but, unlike the other two bosses from hell, the glory-stealer can appear charming and pleasant – while all the while stealing your ideas behind your back. Thus, it can take time to realize what is happening – and it can be hard to take action against a boss who appears to be so nice.

However, perhaps your boss isn't as bad as the three described today, but still causes you concern. Tomorrow, then, we look at solutions to other common boss-related problems.

SUNDAY

MONDAY

TUESDAY

WEDNESDAY

THURSDAY

FRIDAY

SATURDAY

Fact-check (answers at the back)

1. Bullying includes (select the one that does *not* apply)...
   a) Persistent criticism ❑
   b) Personal abuse ❑
   c) Only behaviours occurring in public ❑
   d) Behaviours occurring in public and in private ❑

2. Examples of bullying behaviour from your boss might include...
   a) Picking on you ❑
   b) Humiliating you ❑
   c) Belittling your achievements ❑
   d) Publically criticizing you if you are late. ❑

3. Workplace bullying can cause...
   a) High stress ❑
   b) Dread of work ❑
   c) Schizophrenia ❑
   d) Mental health problems ❑

4. How many adults have been subjected to bullying at some point in their working lives?
   a) 100% ❑
   b) 25% ❑
   c) 50% ❑
   d) 75% ❑

5. Why might your boss bully? Pick one that is not true.
   a) Because they may have been Bullied as a child) ❑
   b) Because they are envious of you ❑
   c) Because they feel threatened by you ❑
   d) Because the victim is so annoying ❑

6. To make an official complaint about a bully boss, which of the following do you *not* need to do...
   a) Keep a diary of incidents ❑
   b) Write a company policy on workplace bullying ❑
   c) Locate any witnesses ❑
   d) Put a complaint in writing ❑

7. Which of the following does not constitute sexual harassment?
   a) Unwelcome sexual advances ❑
   b) Standing too close ❑
   c) Display of sexually explicit materials ❑
   d) Asking questions about your family ❑

8. The glory-stealing boss might...
   a) Give you credit where credit is due ❑
   b) Publically praise you for your ideas ❑
   c) Claim responsibility for your successes ❑
   d) Claim responsibility for your failures. ❑

9. The effects of the glory-stealing boss are that they can...
   a) Block promotion ❑
   b) Hinder your career progression ❑
   c) Cause you stress ❑
   d) Sexually harass you ❑

10. Which of the following would *not* suggest that your glory is being stolen by your boss?
    a) Ideas that they reject appear under their name later on ❑
    b) You are expected to put your boss's name first on any reports you write ❑
    c) Other people know nothing about your achievements ❑
    d) Senior management praise you for your successes ❑

SATURDAY

Managing the boss – common problems

By this point, you should be very well equipped to manage your boss in most everyday situations – as well as deal with the boss from hell, should you be unlucky enough to encounter one. Most of the material this far as been concerned with *proactive* boss management – that is, going out and making a conscious effort to improve the relationship that you have with your boss. However, sometimes, you will need to take a more *reactive* approach by taking action when a situation occurs. Today we look at a more reactive approach to boss management by considering a range of the most common scenarios that require reactive input.

Today, then, we will discuss solutions to these common problems:

- My boss relies on me too much
- I am better at the job than my boss
- My boss is having an affair and I have to cover for them
- My boss expects me to run errands for them
- My boss promised me a rise/promotion but it hasn't materialized
- My boss never tells me what's going on
- My boss doesn't seem to like me
- My boss used to be my colleague – I can't get used to him/her being the boss!
- My boss is a control freak!

My boss relies on me too much

This is a common situation experienced by many PAs (personal assistants) and secretaries, but could happen to anyone. The whole point of your boss being the boss is that they get to delegate work to you and, in extreme cases, have you do the work while they manage the process. It is only a small jump from delegation to total reliance. Your boss may rely on you too much if:

- they always asking your advice
- they expect you to stay late when they do to help them out
- you have to prepare all their presentations for them
- they ring you at home (or on holiday) during your annual leave
- you find that you are not only doing the work, but managing the process, too
- you think you are doing more than your boss
- you organize their work life for them
- they try to block any ideas you have of moving on.

IT'S YOUR BOSS

On the one hand, having your boss rely on you so much can be beneficial to you – making yourself indispensable is a good way of avoiding redundancy and strengthening your bargaining position for a rise. However, it could soon be that you are trapped in a gilded cage – well paid, but unable to move on. Your boss may be so unwilling for you to leave that they go so far as to block promotion prospects or scupper references for you. If you think you are in danger of having a boss rely on you too much, follow these guidelines:

1 **Try and reduce your boss's reliance on you.** Do this by showing your boss how to do some of the tasks you do. Explain that they should know how to do them in case you are ill or unavailable. When projects are discussed, ensure a division of labour by stating that you will do x, y and z if they do a, b and c.

2 **Ensure your prospects are not blocked.** If you do decide it's time to move on, reassure your boss that you will help train up your successor and that you won't leave them in the lurch.

3 **Be non-contactable on leave.** Make sure you take all your leave and prime your boss well in terms of dealing with things in your absence. Then, don't give them your contact details. And, don't ring in either!

I am better at the job than my boss

This is a very different problem from being relied upon too much and requires rather different management. Whereas the over-reliant boss recognizes and accepts your skills, the 'not-as-good-as-me' boss usually does not – and, if they do, they are likely (quite naturally) to feel threatened. It often takes a specific trigger for an employee to realize that they are better at the job than their boss. Such triggers commonly include:

● covering the boss for maternity leave / sick leave – and realizing that you did a better job than they did
● repeated higher achievements than your boss – more sales, awards, publications, etc.
● realization that others come to you for advice/help – not your boss.

The trick to managing this boss is to subtly reassure them that their job is not at risk (even if it is) while ensuring your own deserved advancement – a difficult balance! Quite clearly, if you can do the job better than the boss, then you should be aiming for promotion – to their position or equivalent. However, this does not mean that you should be trying to oust your boss. On the contrary, people move on much more quickly these days than in the days of a 'job for life' (except, perhaps, in some older, more traditional industries), so keeping good relations with your boss may ensure that they will recommend you as their successor. If you do expect your boss to move on in the next couple of years, be patient, bury your frustration and make sure they know what an ideal successor you would make!

But, what if your boss has been there years – and is likely to stay until retirement (and they're only 40)? In this case, you might be better looking for advancement either elsewhere in the company or with a different organization.

You will need to follow the tips elsewhere in this book to ensure you stay on good terms with your boss so that they give you an excellent reference.

My boss is having an affair and I have to cover for them

This is a very tricky situation made worse by the following circumstances:

- you know/are friendly with the boss's spouse/partner
- you are asked to lie to the spouse/partner
- you are expected to lie to other people at work.

How do you manage this boss? Do you lie and keep your boss happy, or refuse to cover for them and risk their wrath – and the consequences of that for your career? The answer depends, in part, on your attitude to the whole thing. Some people take the view that what their boss (or anyone else) gets up to is not their concern, and refuse to moralize. If you are happy to cover for your boss when their spouse/partner calls, then go ahead. However, many people do feel uncomfortable with lying to anyone, especially the partner of someone having an affair. Use the following guide to manage a cheating boss:

1 **Sit down with your boss.** You need to explain to them how uncomfortable lying makes you feel without actually refusing to do it. Ask them if there is another way – perhaps your boss could persuade their partner not to call them at work or maybe they could agree to lie to you about their whereabouts so that you can tell the 'truth' to the spouse/partner!

2 **Resist the urge to moralize or lecture.** You may be entitled not to want to lie, but it is not your place to teach your boss right from wrong (which they are probably well aware of anyway).

3 If you cannot reach an agreement with your boss over this, **you will have to decide what matters more to you** – your current job or a blemish on your integrity. It might be that, if you can ride it out, the affair will peter out before too long; but, if not, you may want to think about moving on. After all, you may feel that you no longer want to work for someone who not only lies and cheats on their partner, but doesn't respect your wish not to be involved.

My boss expects me to run errands for them

It's one thing running out for the occasional sandwich for your boss, but it's quite another being expected to collect their dry-cleaning, buy a birthday present for their partner, book theatre tickets and do their Christmas shopping! However, in managing this kind of boss, it is important to weigh up a number of considerations. Ask yourself the following questions:

● **What is my job title?** A Personal Assistant could reasonably be expected to do some personal errands if it frees up time for your boss to concentrate on their job. But it is less reasonable to expect this of an Assistant Personnel Manager.

● **Is my boss otherwise reasonable?** If so, perhaps the errand-running could be put up with as a minor irritation.

● **Am I gaining valuable experience/training in this job?** It is definitely worth putting up with these inconveniences if, in the grand scale of things, you are advancing your career.

● **Does the time taken doing errands eat into the time I have available for doing my job?** If so, this suggests the errand-running is getting out of hand.

● **Am I having to stay late to fit in their errands and my own work?** You definitely need to tackle your boss!

If, having asked yourself the above questions, you decide that you cannot put up and shut up for much longer, it is time to tackle your boss. The angle to take is the infringement on your work quality that running their errands is producing. Explain that, while you are happy to run the occasional errand, you are being paid to do another job and you are unable to do it justice when you are constantly interrupted by having to do things that are not part of your work. Your boss may not be aware just how much time you do spend on their errands, so it might be useful to keep a time sheet so that they can see that the 'odd errand' is actually taking up more than five hours a week.

My boss promised me a rise/ promotion but it hasn't materialized

This is a surprisingly common problem. The boss implicitly or explicitly leads you to believe that a rise or promotion will be yours, only to 'forget' having ever promised it – or to say that you misunderstood what they said. Usually, the promise is in return for your working late or completing a piece of work particularly well. Or it is a promise made in order to retain you through turbulent or difficult times.

If this has happened to you, there is little you can do this time to force your boss's hand. But you can learn from the experience. Next time you are made any kind of promise, follow this guide:

1 **Make it explicit.** Promises of rises or promotions are often implied suggestions (e.g. 'If we win this contract, I'll see you right' or 'It will be very much in your interest to complete this project'). It is important to make these suggestions explicit by asking for clarification. Ask your boss exactly what they mean by 'in your interest' or 'seeing you right'. If they are vague, ask if this means a rise or promotion. Ask what kind of promotion or what sort of figure the rise would be.
2 **Put it in writing.** Send a (dated) memo to your boss in which you express your delight in being offered the rise/promotion to be awarded at the end of the project/when the piece of work is completed.
3 **Follow-up.** Once the piece of work is completed (or whatever you had to do before the offered rise was awarded), ask your boss for what was promised.

My boss never tells me what's going on

Your boss is not, of course, obliged to tell you everything that is going on, but it does make your work life more pleasant if you are kept informed of the things that effect you. Your boss may be unreasonably keeping things from you if:

- you are suddenly moved to a different office with no prior warning
- you see an advert in the paper for a new position in your firm – working alongside you
- there are rumours of a merger but your boss won't say anything
- you hear important things on the grapevine before you do from your boss
- people in other departments know more about company changes than you do.

The best way to manage the 'information-retentive' boss is to join forces with your colleagues (since they are likely to be just as irritated). If you cannot get others to join you (perhaps you are in a small firm or department), then you can still go it alone. Either way, the following guide should help:

1 **Gather some evidence.** Complaining vaguely to your boss about not being kept informed won't carry much weight. If, however, you can give several examples of incidents when you were not told about something (that you feel was unreasonably withheld), you will have a stronger case.

2 **Explain why you are bothered.** Some withholding of information can just be irritating but there are occasions when it can make a practical difference. You should tell your boss how you felt and about the result that the lack of information has/had on your morale, work output or modus operandi (for instance, perhaps if you had known about something you could have prepared in advance and thus wasted less work time).

3 **Emphasize the positives.** Try to avoid simply presenting your boss with criticism. Explain that you are very enthusiastic about the way they do something else (e.g. assigns work, gives feedback, etc.). This should greatly increase your chances of success!

My boss doesn't seem to like me

Your boss does not *have* to like you. As long as they respect the job you do, they do not have to want to be your best buddy. However, we all know that it can help enormously if your boss does like you since they will be more likely to:

- do favours for you
- grant your requests
- make allowances when necessary
- make your working conditions pleasurable
- give you desirable tasks.

How do you know if your boss does not like you? Most of us instinctively know when someone dislikes us, but here are some clues to look out for:

- your boss doesn't smile at you (but he does at your colleagues)
- your boss seems irritated by you
- your boss seems to avoid you
- your boss gives you the least desirable tasks
- your boss rarely grants requests or favours.

The best way to manage this boss is to try and find out what it is that they dislike about you. But be warned! This honesty should only be sought if you can take it.

Rather than ask your boss straight out why they dislike you (which is certain to elicit denials from your boss since no one wants to be downright offensive), it is more effective to ask them if there is anything that you are doing (or not doing) that they would rather were different. The best time to ask this is at your annual appraisal, but if yours is a long way off, you could find another opportunity. If your boss is reluctant to be drawn into talking about your faults, help them out by making a couple of suggestions. If you do manage to tease out the reason, see if you can change whatever it is that is causing the problem. At the end of the day, however, it could just be a personality clash between the two of you and you may have to accept this – or move on.

My boss used to be my colleague – I can't get used to him/her being my boss!

There are all sorts of issues tied up in this problem. It is almost inevitable that at some point in your working life a colleague will get promoted and become your superior. This can be difficult for both of you to cope with. You may feel jealous and resentful that they got promoted over you. They, on the other hand, may find it tough to be a 'boss' while not appearing to be 'lording' it over former friends and colleagues. This plan should guide you:

1 **Your colleague is the boss now – get used to it!** Any feelings of resentment you have need to be swallowed or put to one side – they are destructive and your career could suffer. Maybe your colleague did not deserve the promotion – there's nothing you can do about it so you may as well put up and shut up. Attempting to sabotage your new boss's progress is more likely to backfire on you.
2 **Be honest.** Tell your new boss how awkward you feel with the new balance of power. The chances are, they probably feel the same way. Once these feelings are out in the open, you can discuss and agree new ground rules (e.g. whether you will continue to eat together in the canteen, drink together after work, etc.).

3 **Be on your their side.** The best way to manage this particular boss is to help them and generally be there for them. They will probably be finding the transition difficult, too, and will be forever grateful to you for making life easier at this time.

4 **Don't be too matey!** Be very careful not to go too far in your attempts to keep on the good side of your new boss. Being too friendly can have its downside, too, as work and social boundaries become blurred. A mate for a boss can easily take advantage of you by asking you to do 'favours' (such as continually working late or at weekends) that you find it harder to say 'no' to than you would to a boss who was never your friend socially. It is important for both of you to maintain a business separation – even if this is something that can be switched off at the end of the working day.

My boss is a control freak!

You know your boss is a control freak when:

- they find it almost impossible to delegate
- they are so involved with your work that they might as well be doing it
- they want to know everything that you are doing
- they insist on everything being done their way
- they ring in three times a day while on vacation
- they rarely take their full leave
- they want constant reports from you.

The only way to manage the control freak boss is to build up their confidence by playing to their obsession. The controlling boss is terrified to let go, because, if they do, their world might fall apart. You need to convince them that this will not be so – that not only will their world continue to function, but that it will function very well. You will only be able to achieve this through time and by using the following tips:

- Pre-empt your boss's need to check up on you by supplying regular reports and updates.
- Keep in regular communication with your boss so that they don't need to contact you.
- Do the work exactly how the boss tells you – resist introducing your own way of doing things (yet).
- Don't pester for or demand more freedom.
- Make sure you know the exact state of play of projects in readiness for when your boss asks.
- Do work in a logical fashion which will appeal to your boss's need for order.

If you follow these tips for several months (or longer), your boss may eventually learn to trust you. Control freaks do often have one or two people whom they feel it is safe to delegate to, but once you become one of them, be sure to continue to behave as before. The only difference is that you might be able to start suggesting or introducing small changes. The controlling boss is not afraid of change, just of being out of control, so make sure any change involves and includes them – it's even better if you can make them think it was their idea!

Summary

Today, then, we ended the week by discussing nine of the most common problems that you are likely to encounter with your boss at work. We have considered step-by-step approaches to each issue and, in doing so, should have covered almost every common difficulty that you might encounter. Dealing with these scenarios in a positive way can turn a potentially major source of conflict into something much more manageable.

Even if you haven't yet encountered any of the problems outlined here, it is worth bearing them in mind – since forewarned is forearmed, after all. The chances are that at some point in your working life you will meet one or more of these difficulties.

By now, your toolbox of skills should be such that you are able to manage your boss both proactively and reactively and from the very first encounter. With time and practice, you should become adept at managing your boss and at developing a strong, positive and mutually beneficial relationship.

SUNDAY
MONDAY
TUESDAY
WEDNESDAY
THURSDAY
FRIDAY
SATURDAY

Fact-check (answers at the back)

1. You know your boss relies on you too much when (select the one that does not apply)...
   a) They are always asking your advice ☐
   b) You have to prepare their reports and presentations ☐
   c) They ring you constantly when you are on leave ☐
   d) They always criticize your work ☐

2. You know you are better at the job than your boss when (select the one that does not apply)...
   a) You covered for them when they were sick and did the job better ☐
   b) You have higher achievements than your boss (e.g. more sales) ☐
   c) You stay later at the office than they do ☐
   d) People come to you for advice, not to your boss ☐

3. Your boss is having an affair and expects you to cover for them. You should deal with this by...
   a) Refusing to cover for them ☐
   b) Lying for them to their partner ☐
   c) Lecturing to your boss about their morals ☐
   d) Explaining how uncomfortable it makes you feel. ☐

4. It is unreasonable for my boss to expect you to...
   a) Fetch a coffee for them ☐
   b) Choose a birthday present for their partner ☐
   c) Collect their dry-cleaning ☐
   d) Work late in order to fit in their errands ☐

5. If you are promised promotion by your boss, which of the following should you *not* do?
   a) Get it in writing ☐
   b) Ask for clarification on the terms ☐
   c) Follow up the promise ☐
   d) Sit back and wait for your promotion ☐

6. Which of the following is *not* a good way to manage the boss who doesn't tell you much?
   a) Join forces with colleagues ☐
   b) Gather evidence ☐
   c) Complain to your boss that they never tell you what's going on ☐
   d) Use specific examples ☐

7. Which of the following is *not* a sign that your boss might not like you?
   a) They rarely smile at you (but do smile at your colleagues) ☐
   b) They expect high standards of you ☐
   c) They give you the least desirable tasks ☐
   d) They rarely grant requests or favours ☐

8. You should cope with a colleague being promoted to your boss by...
   a) Feeling jealous and resentful ☐
   b) Complaining about them behind their back ☐
   c) Telling them how you feel ☐
   d) Treating them like your best friend ☐

9. Which of the following is a sign that your boss is a control freak?
a) They are always delegating ❏
b) They are happy for you to try things your way ❏
c) They are not contactable or in contact when on leave ❏
d) They want to change everything you do ❏

10. Which of the following strategies should you *not* use to manage the control freak boss?
a) Supply them with regular updates ❏
b) Do the main parts of the job their way but the rest your way ❏
c) Build up their trust in you ❏
d) Let them have as much control as they need. ❏

SUNDAY MONDAY TUESDAY WEDNESDAY THURSDAY FRIDAY SATURDAY

Surviving in tough times

In these tough economic climes it has never been more important to manage your boss effectively. In better times, if we landed the boss from hell, we had the option of deciding to cut our losses and find another job. Today, with fewer alterative jobs available, such possibilities are often severely limited. So, now that quitting is a less feasible option for most of us, getting on with the boss is more crucial than ever before. And yet there are potentially more reasons than ever before for not getting on with your boss, since the austere climate we find ourselves in is likely to contribute greatly to the stress and pressure at work. Here, then, are ten crucial tips to help you manage your boss:

1 Don't wait – start managing your boss now!

It is all too easy to put off 'boss management' until you have a problem but, in these difficult times, we never know what is around the corner. Everyone is under more pressure at work and this may mean that even a great boss whom you have always got on well with is having to adopt unpopular policies and strategies that might cause you difficulties. Or, as is happening more and more these days, the boss that you know and love might leave or take a different position – meaning you have a new, unknown entity in charge. Either way, the best strategy for you is to start managing your boss today!

2 Impression management is everything!

Creating and maintaining a good impression is the most important boss-management strategy and this is more important than ever when times are tough. Bosses having to employ unpopular austerity measures are likely to meet increasing hostility from their staff, but it is important to remember that your boss is fighting for the firm's survival. Their tough stance is probably necessary so working hard on managing the hostility and instead showing support for your boss is likely to be appreciated.

3 Work out your boss's leadership style

In these difficult times your boss may have to take on tough new roles, which means that their management style may change. A previously consultative boss may, by necessity, become more dictatorial as fewer concessions are available. So, even if you thought you knew how your boss managed their staff, use this book to keep in tune with any changing styles of leadership that might result from the changing economic climate.

4 Spend time on your psychological contract

The psychological contract covers all those unwritten agreements to do with such issues as working patterns (for example, expectations about working from home or flexi-work), levels of proactivity (such as whether you are expected to seek work or wait for it to come in) and professional development (such as training availability). In these difficult times the rules in many of these areas may have changed so revisiting the psychological contract is very beneficial.

5 Establish your boss's communication style

In this instance, communication style refers to how your boss likes to be communicated with – using email or face-to-face meetings, with regular updates or only where troubleshooting is required, and so on. Whereas previously your boss may have expected frequent face-to-faces with the team, today's more austere climate might mean that the rules have changed and there is no longer the time for such luxuries. Finding out how your boss prefers to be kept up to speed can make the difference between annoying them or making life easier for them.

6 Figure out what makes your boss tick

Everyone has a 'thinking style' and working out how your boss thinks means that you can make efforts to work in a way that concurs with this thinking style. In today's tough climate when time and resources are so precious, saving your boss time by working in a way that works with and not against the way their brain processes information can only help them – and thus, you!

7 Be professional!

When so many of us are having to accomplish more work with fewer resources in these austere times, it is easy to consider cutting corners. But the key to successful management of the boss is to always be professional, so this is one area where corner-cutting is not beneficial. Being professional, which means being punctual, appropriately dressed, meeting deadlines and ensuring work looks great, should not be compromised even when times are tough.

8 Don't be afraid of being assertive

When times are tough and redundancies threaten, it is easy to fall into the trap of lying low and not wanting to rock the boat. Being assertive with your boss is even more important in difficult times when your boss is more likely to want to offload more work on to you than is reasonable due to staffing and resource shortages. Standing up for yourself in these times is essential and this book has shown you how to achieve this without marking you out for redundancy!

9 Don't put up with a boss from hell

In these difficult economic times when redundancies abound, many of us are grateful for a job – any job. This means that we are more likely to put up with the boss from hell than in times when there is a greater possibility of finding alternative employment. However, the choices are not simply between putting up and moving on – managing the boss from hell is a realistic option, too. And, because it is harder to walk away than ever before, it is more important to manage the relationship with your boss even when things seem like they have escalated to irredeemable levels.

10 Make life as easy for your boss as possible

The final tip has to be this: the easier you make life for your boss, the better your relationship with them is likely to be. When times are tough for us all, they are just as tough for the manager who has to make difficult decisions in order to maintain financial security. You can make things easier for them by continuing to meet and exceed their expectations, even when it might be harder to do so. It is also worth looking for ways that you can lighten their load if at all possible – if you show that you are on their side, they are more likely to be on your side when it really matters.

Answers

Sunday: 1a; 2c; 3d; 4c; 5a; 6a; 7c; 8c; 9b; 10c

Monday: 1a; 2c; 3c; 4d; 5c; 6a; 7a; 8b; 9d; 10c

Tuesday: 1c; 2d; 3d; 4c; 5a; 6a; 7d; 8c; 9c; 10c

Wednesday: 1a; 2d; 3c; 4a; 5b; 6d; 7d; 8c; 9d; 10b

Thursday: 1d; 2c; 3c; 4b; 5a; 6d; 7a; 8a; 9a; 10d

Friday: 1c; 2d; 3c; 4b; 5d; 6b; 7d; 8c; 9d; 10d

Saturday: 1d; 2c; 3d; 4a; 5d; 6c; 7b; 8c; 9d; 10b

Useful books and websites

Pearson, P., *Keeping Well at Work: A TUC Guide*, 2nd edn (London: Kogan Page, 2004). This is a general book on health and wellbeing at work and includes much focus on legal issues and 'rights' rather than psychological processes. However, it has interesting sections on stress and bullying.

Peyton, P.R., *Dignity at Work: Eliminate Bullying and Create a Positive Working Environment* (Hove: Brunner-Routledge, 2003)

Acas has a good site: www.acas.org.uk/index. aspx?articleid=797

Otherwise SupportLine: www.supportline.org.uk/problems/ bullying_at_work.php

The Andrea Adams Trust: www.workplacebullying.co.uk/ index.html

References

Adams, A. (1992). *Bullying at Work and How to Confront It* (London: Virago Press)

Rayner, C. (1997). 'The incidence of workplace bullying', *Journal of Community and Applied Social Psychology* 7: 199–208

Le Poidevin, J. (1996). 'Tackling workplace bullies', *IRS Employment Review* 611: 11–13

Randall, P. (1997). *Adult Bullying: Perpetrators and Victims* (London: Routledge)

Savva, C. and Alexandrou, A. (1998). 'The impact of bullying in further and higher education', paper presented to the *Bullying at Work, 1998 Research Update Conference*, Staffordshire University, Stafford, 1 July

Notes

ALSO AVAILABLE IN THE 'IN A WEEK' SERIES

BODY LANGUAGE FOR MANAGEMENT • BOOKKEEPING AND ACCOUNTING • CUSTOMER CARE • SPEED READING • DEALING WITH DIFFICULT PEOPLE • EMOTIONAL INTELLIGENCE • FINANCE FOR NON-FINANCIAL MANAGERS • INTRODUCING MANAGEMENT • MANAGING YOUR BOSS • MARKET RESEARCH • NEURO-LINGUISTIC PROGRAMMING • OUTSTANDING CREATIVITY • PLANNING YOUR CAREER • SUCCEEDING AT INTERVIEWS • SUCCESSFUL APPRAISALS • SUCCESSFUL ASSERTIVENESS • SUCCESSFUL BUSINESS PLANS • SUCCESSFUL CHANGE MANAGEMENT • SUCCESSFUL COACHING • SUCCESSFUL COPYWRITING • SUCCESSFUL CVS • SUCCESSFUL INTERVIEWING

For information about other titles in the series, please visit
www.inaweek.co.uk

ALSO AVAILABLE IN THE 'IN A WEEK' SERIES

SUCCESSFUL JOB APPLICATIONS • SUCCESSFUL JOB HUNTING • SUCCESSFUL KEY ACCOUNT MANAGEMENT • SUCCESSFUL LEADERSHIP • SUCCESSFUL MARKETING • SUCCESSFUL MARKETING PLANS • SUCCESSFUL MEETINGS • SUCCESSFUL MEMORY TECHNIQUES • SUCCESSFUL MENTORING • SUCCESSFUL NEGOTIATING • SUCCESSFUL NETWORKING • SUCCESSFUL PEOPLE SKILLS • SUCCESSFUL PRESENTING • SUCCESSFUL PROJECT MANAGEMENT • SUCCESSFUL PSYCHOMETRIC TESTING • SUCCESSFUL PUBLIC RELATIONS • SUCCESSFUL RECRUITMENT • SUCCESSFUL SELLING • SUCCESSFUL STRATEGY • SUCCESSFUL TIME MANAGEMENT • TACKLING INTERVIEW QUESTIONS

For information about other titles in the series, please visit www.inaweek.co.uk

LEARN IN A WEEK,
WHAT THE EXPERTS
LEARN IN A LIFETIME

For information about other titles
in the series, please visit
www.inaweek.co.uk